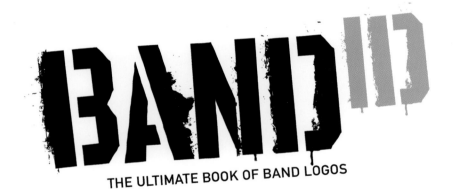

# BAND ID

## THE ULTIMATE BOOK OF BAND LOGOS

BY BODHI OSER

FOREWORD BY ART CHANTRY

CHRONICLE BOOKS

SAN FRANCISCO

LIBRARY OF CONGRESS CATALOGING-IN-PUBLICATION DATA AVAILABLE.

ISBN: 978-0-8118-6049-9

MANUFACTURED IN CHINA

DESIGNED BY BODHI OSER

THANK YOU TO ALL OF THE DESIGNERS AND RECORD COMPANIES THAT MADE THIS BOOK POSSIBLE.

SPECIAL THANKS TO: ART CHANTRY, JOHN PASCHE, GERARD HUERTA, TOM JERMANN, INVISIBLE CREATURE, CHRIS BILHEIMER, HENRIK WALSE, GREGG BERNSTEIN, JASON MUNN, KARLSSONWILKER INC., SLANG INC., MORNINGBREATH INC., SOPP COLLECTIVE, RED DESIGN, AND KHYBER OSER.

10 9 8 7 6 5 4 3 2 1

CHRONICLE BOOKS LLC

680 SECOND STREET

SAN FRANCISCO, CALIFORNIA 94107

WWW.CHRONICLEBOOKS.COM

# TABLE OF CONTENTS

# BANDS HAVE LOGOS?

BY ART CHANTRY

Every time I showed off the galleys of this book, the immediate reaction was, "Bands have logos?" I was examining it in a coffee shop and a small crowd of strangers hovered over my shoulder, all expressing surprise and wonder at the rock logos. They were thrilled to see them, but they all said, "Bands have logos?"

*Of course* bands have logos. Rock bands are carefully defined corporate entities. Think about the Rolling Stones' tongue logo, or the Grateful Dead's skull-and-lightning-bolt logo. Or the Beatles. Or the Monkees. Or the Sex Pistols. You bet they have logos. They're on millions of T-shirts and posters and record covers and God knows what. I'll bet you know somebody who has Black Flag's emblem tattooed on their body. How many corporate logos can you think of that someone would permanently apply to their skin? Name one. (Well, actually, the photographer Charles Peterson has a Leica logo on his forearm, but he's a special case.)

Few things in popular culture (or "trash culture," as I personally prefer) become as visible, as ubiquitous, and as universal as a rock band logo. Band logos denote personal allegiance and expression. They define the tribe of fandom. When you see kids wearing T-shirts with the Misfits' crimson skull logo, they are telling you exactly where they stand, and what they like, and, more exactingly, what they *don't* like (i.e.—you). They are also isolating themselves into a marginal definition of self. They are using the icon to give themselves a personal identity that they attempt to build a life around. You did the same thing when you drew that AC/DC logo on your high school yearbook and carried it around. It tied you into the culture you wanted to belong to. In the end, it helped form your adulthood. Try to make *that* claim with an Exxon logo.

When you first picked up this book, I'll bet good money that at first you responded with a thrill to each favorite band you randomly encountered. Then you probably looked for some of your favorite logos pulled from memory. (*Did they get the Dolls in there? How about Yes?*) I imagine you might have even turned to the index to see if your band is listed. Sophisticated aficionados possibly tried to find the work of specific designers. We all have our favorite logos and we already know them well enough not only to identify them at a glance, but to reproduce them. They are so well-known and simultaneously so subconscious that we already have them burned into our brains, and if given a pencil, I'll bet you could actually draw them fairly accurately. Go ahead, try it. Draw the Kiss logo. I'll bet you can.

These logos define tribes. Band logos became symbols even more powerful than the music the bands created—they became iconographic symbols of defiance and rebellion and rebirth and belonging. The Stones' tongue still makes you wince and chuckle thirty years later. The black metal logos are completely illegible, and as a result they frighten you. They are sloppy, chaotic images that are more illustrations than words, but the inherent message they ram home is, "Stay away. This is not for you." Many logos in these rock subcultures are more accurately described as anti-logos designed to attract only the chosen. They are also designed to keep the uninitiated at bay—"no trespassing." They seem more like open wounds than logos.

Gary Panter's logo for the greatest unrecorded punk band of all time, the Screamers, is a wonderful case in point. When his modern-angst-driven, biting/attacking/screaming illustration of lead singer Tomata du Plenty hit the streets of Los Angeles, it changed the underground world. This was 1977.

THE SCREAMERS / GARY PANTER / 1977

*Star Wars* and *Saturday Night Fever* were both still in theaters, and the visual rock world was all disco chrome and stadiums—a tired, shallow, exhausted, cynical, pointless product. Suddenly this *face* was screaming directly at you from every telephone pole in town, this horrible pitiless angry screaming *face*. Everybody's reaction was shock—"What the hell is that?!?" It was a sort of primal scream therapy for a generation. This single image unleashed a mutant horde of frustrated, disenfranchised outsider youths desperate for a world, any world, that they could possibly fit into. This single face spread across the nation (and beyond) with a life of its own. It brought punk psychodrama to mainstream populations for the first time, going far beyond the provincial urban capsules of New York City and London. It sparked an underground revolution. It was not just an insignia; it was a call to arms.

In the earlier days of the Seattle underground music scene, there was one rock band that used a logo instead of a name (this was years before Prince went abstract). The mark was two diamond shapes colliding into one form with a bat wing on either side. It was a "flying double-diamond bat thing." It was on street flyers everywhere. According to fans, the name of the band was pronounced like a scream: "AIIIIIIIEEEEEEEEEE..........." The band developed a large but peculiar following. In those experimental days, when anything was considered worth try-ing and generally was, such a ploy (though self-conscious and cloying) actually spoke to a large segment of the underground population. It actually worked. The power of a clever logo to initiate the like-minded into the fold cannot be underestimated here. It can be used to filter, separate, and then capture the "others who think like you." It is a rally point for subculture.

Then there is the confusion factor. Many of these logos are cultural parody. I imagine there is a large percentage of the population who, when confronted with the seal of the President of the United States of America, think it's the Ramones' logo. Some may even giggle when they see President Bush standing behind a podium with the Ramones' logo on the front. Maybe some think he's an old punk rocker. Things get so confusing in these days of postmodern appropriation that I wonder.

It wasn't always this way. Rock bands as legitimate business identities didn't emerge until the early 1960s, nearly ten years after the genre evolved. Elvis never had a logo. Probably the very first important corporate rock logo was for the Beatles. It was the original pioneer of corporate rock marketing. It sold a bazillion products, each of them with an official brand imprint. It was the seed. The psychedelic era nailed down corporate logos and the '70s expanded them to gross proportions. Punk rebelled against the corporate takeover of the music and adopted anti-logos. Punk trashed it all and the symbols became tribal, closer to outlaw motorcycle gangs than brand identities.

Still, it's hard to imagine that H.R. Giger—the man who designed *Alien* and countless *Necronomicon* images—actually designed a rather mechanical and soulless mark for Emerson, Lake & Palmer. It looks more like an icon for Devo or Kraftwerk. (Why did he do that?) The Sex Pistols' logo was actually cre-ated by a member of the infamous Bromley Contingent, Helen Worthington-Smith (the little person last seen in *The Great Rock and Roll Swindle* dragging the logo behind her on a long rope).

Jamie Reid, the master Situationist designer, simply took her work off an existing flyer and re-presented it, and it became history, with a total disregard for any corporate standards. Nirvana's logo was created through a lack of money (total payment: $15) and a convenient collaboration between two people with tired, cynical attitudes. The typeface was chosen because it happened to be on the typesetting machine at the moment the bored designer asked the bored type guy to set some type for free. I wonder how many millions in rock swag have been sold with that logo? The "whacked happy face" you see in this book was actually lifted (photocopied) from a button advertising a local Seattle strip club.

Of course, there are those countless chrome-encrusted, jagged, and nasty metal logos (Metallica, Slayer, Judas Priest, Van Halen, AC/DC), and clean, attractive arena-rock corporate marks (Journey, Asia, Chicago, even the Carpenters). It's no wonder punk formed as a D.I.Y. rejection of business and design sensibilities. Any level of talent or skill was acceptable. The point was to make it yourself, to participate and help destroy (or at least redefine) the world. The repetition of the early marks on posters and cheap 45 covers was an accident of convenience rather than an actual planned design effort. That was what they had, so they copied them and reused them. Those punk logos became logos by necessity. The fact that many of the anti-logos today carry recognition far in excess of the carefully drawn, expensively reproduced corporate IDs of so many bands that sold so many more records is a testament to their pertinence and intellectual insight. A good logo says everything it needs to say symbolically, and lousy reproduction can't change that.

Band logos and identities have been a part of popular culture for over half a century. It's high time we recognized them and gave them the attention they have deserved for so long. I seriously doubt any of the logos in this book ever won a design award or were collected in major museums. This is the stuff of a different sensibility. It's a living, breathing, throbbing world that they inhabit. Without them we probably wouldn't be who we are today. This is some of the most important popular design of the last half-century, all of it gone undocumented and unrecorded. That is, until now. At last, band logos getting the respect they richly deserve. It's time to toast your favorites. Use beer.

# INTRODUCTION

I'm not an expert on this subject.

I'm just a graphic designer and music fan who was surprised to find out that a book on band logos didn't already exist. When an L.A. band hired me to create their new logo recently, I did what I usually do when I get a new project: I swung by the Hennessey & Ingalls bookstore in Santa Monica to scan all the graphic design books for ideas and inspiration. There were plenty of books on CD packaging, plus a wide range on album covers, rock posters, and concert T-shirts, along with a heap on general logo design—but not a single book solely devoted to the art of band logo design. So I decided I'd make one.

My hippie parents are huge music fans, so I was lucky to grow up with an eclectic mixture of rock, jazz, folk, and funk playing in the house. My dad also took me to amazing concerts at an early age: the Dead, Springsteen, the Bee Gees, Billy Joel, and a bunch of other '70s bands in their prime. I was sitting seventh row center for "The Boss" while my friends were watching the mechanical band at the local Chuck E. Cheese. By the early '80s I was going to shows by myself, at first to bands like Journey and Men at Work. Then came the Van Halen *1984* tour, and I became a guitar and hard rock junkie, moving full-on into '80s hair metal trash bands like Cinderella, Britny Fox, and others that I'm not (that) afraid to admit to liking. I also had a totally fucked-up-looking curly mullet (see inset photo, circa 1988). But it was the next big concert I saw that changed everything (again); Ozzy, at the Philly Spectrum. I was dropped off with my friend Shon Pistol (what a rock 'n' roll name, even!). I'd never heard of the opening band, Metallica, but as soon as they walked on stage and ripped into "Battery," I instantly became a die-hard heavy metal fan. Those glam bands were dead to me, and now I only liked the heavy shit: Slayer, Venom, Possessed. . . I would've been totally sucked into the all-metal vortex

if it wasn't for my skater friends. For some reason, listening to metal was cool when I was into BMX, but as soon as I traded in the bike for a skateboard I was also introduced to Bad Brains, Dead Kennedys, and Suicidal Tendencies, and my musical tastes just kept expanding.

This was also high school, which I hated, spending most of my time scribbling Van Halen, Metallica, and Dead Kennedys logos on my notebooks instead of paying attention in class. Perfecting the shading and angles of the wings on the VH logo was much more interesting than algebra. (I'm pretty sure that this had a big part in my eventually becoming a designer.) I wasn't the only one who scribbled these logos in notebooks or carved them into desks. Attaching yourself to a band's identity was a big part of demonstrating your own identity. Because I'd gone to so many concerts for so many years, I also had a pretty rad concert-tee collection. For a while that's all I wore every day. I'd proudly sport my Slayer tees down the hall to let everyone know "Hey! I'm the type of person that listens to Slayer, so I'm a fucking bad-ass," and then the next day to switch it up, I'd wear a Prince shirt. Then I was saying, "See, I like Slayer and Prince. I'm so diverse, and mysterious." That's really all it takes to communicate to someone what kind of person you want to be seen as—a band logo on a T-shirt. If you're wearing a Cannibal Corpse logo, you're distinguishing yourself as a completely different type of person than the guy in a Phish shirt, who's broadcasting his own identity as a stoner hippie loser (sorry, Phish guy . . . ).

Despite liking all sorts of music, I am a metalhead at heart, and I guess I always have been. You may see this in the forthcoming logo selection. I've tried to keep things balanced, but honestly, metal (followed by punk and hip-hop) has paid more attention to the power of the iconic logo than other genres of music.

Regrettably, one of the things I discovered in working on this book is that band logos as an art form seem to be dying. Sure, bands definitely do still have logos, but more often than not, bands change their graphic identities from album to album now. Nobody's sticking to one identity anymore like they used to (except the metal bands— they hold on to their logos longer than their leather pants). Even if the famous AC/DC logo was a different color on every album, or there was a drop-shadow on it, or it was outlined, it was still the same design, and it was instantly recognizable. I think that's what has made some logos "classics," and others more forgettable. The smart bands were also smart brands, and they plastered the same identity on merchandise for years. If we close our eyes and think of the Top 10 most memorable band logos, they're ones the bands kept using album after album.

Not only is the band logo fighting the current short-attention-span zeitgeist, but we've also traded the 12-inch album canvas for a 4.75-inch CD booklet, and now even these are evaporating into MP3s, just names written in Helvetica to scroll through on our iPods. (Teensy digital thumbnails of the album covers? Please.) You could go to the band's Web site, or sport one of its T-shirts, but these designs are changing with each album now, too.

I offer this book as a tribute to the artists who created these icons, and to the bands who made them famous. I've made every effort to show the cleanest, most commonly used version of each logo. Some I got from the original designers (when I could locate them), some came from other designers who re-created the logos for use on various projects, and many of them I re-created myself. Many of these logos were originally created by hand in a pre-digital age. I did my best.

In addition to the canonical, iconic logos you'd expect, you'll see that I've included logos that weren't necessarily used over and over through the years by the band, but may have become iconic through a single enduring appearance. I've also included some examples that I just think are great logos.

I also wanted this book to be informative, so I've interviewed some of the people who were instrumental in creating these logos we've grown to love. I talked to a good cross-section of designers, musicians, and label heads, and picked their brains about not only their own logos, but also some of the industry "classics." As far as the book's layout, I initially considered going alphabetical (to make it easiest to look up a specific band) but ultimately decided it would be better to organize everything by genre since: a) we're living in an iTunes world now anyway and b) readers can now just check out the Hip-Hop section if that's the only category they're looking for. But as a compromise, I've also included a complete alphabetical index so that it's still easy to quickly look up a certain band by name. Like I said in the beginning, I'm not an expert on this subject, just a fan. Fortunately, my first choice in experts, esteemed designer Art Chantry, was willing to help out on this project, and he was gracious enough to write the book's foreword—a bunch of his logos are in the book and also cover the endsheets. Art was the longtime art director for Estrus Records and possesses an incredible amount of general knowledge on the bands and designers who have shaped these logos over the years.

I know people are going to complain, "Hey, dumbfuck, you forgot the logo for MY FAVORITE BAND." All I can say in response is that I hope that this book might become a living project that can expand into future editions. I've also made every attempt to research and credit all the logo designers I could find, but for a number of them, I was unfortunately unable to identify the original artists (in some cases, perhaps the design came from an anonymous friend of the bassist, or is uncredited work by the drummer's brother). If you are this talented anonymous friend of the bassist, or if anyone else has been miscredited, please e-mail me at contact@bandidbook.com so updates or corrections can be made in the future.

Rock on.

# THE TONGUE

"On 29 April 1970, Jo Bergman, who was running the Stones' office at the time, wrote to me to confirm that they had commissioned me to design a poster for their forthcoming 1970 European Tour. At this time, I was in my final year of a graduate design course at the Royal College of Art in London. I was very honoured when Mick Jagger turned up at the college to see my final degree show. A short time later, I met with Mick again, who asked me to design a logo or symbol for the Rolling Stones' record label. Mick showed me an image of the goddess of Kali, which was the starting point to our discussion regarding the design of the logo. I was paid £50 for the design, which took me about a week to complete. In 1972, I was paid an additional £200 in recognition of the logo's success.

The first use of the logo was the inner sleeve for the *Sticky Fingers* album. The outer sleeve was designed by Warhol, hence the mix-up with the credits. (Warhol has been incorrectly attributed by many sources.) The logo was not fully registered in all countries and a German jeans company registered the logo in Germany for their own products. This situation, and the fact that the Tongue was getting used by unauthorised manufacturers of badges and T-shirts, prompted proper registration and a merchandising agreement with myself to capitalise on the success of the logo.

The design concept for the Tongue was to represent the band's antiauthoritarian attitude, Mick's mouth, and the obvious sexual connotations. I designed it in such a way that it was easily reproduced and in a style that I thought could stand the test of time. Due to its immediate popularity, the Stones kept with it over the years and I believe that it represents one of the strongest and most recognisable logos worldwide. And of course I'm proud of that.

The simplicity of the design lent itself to many variations, which were done by other designers and not myself. The Stones ultimately bought the copyright (in 1982) but I still own the hand-drawn artwork. My busiest time creating artwork for the Stones was from 1970–1974, including four tour posters. This led to work for Paul McCartney, the Who, and many other artists and bands through to eleven years ago when I started working as creative director for the South Bank Centre Arts Complex in London. I left this position last April due to the closure of the Royal Festival Hall for an eighteen-month renovation programme. I am now 60 years old and work as a freelance designer from my studio at home. Still enjoying rock music and working as a designer."

JOHN PASCHE
MAY 2007

ROLLING STONES / ROLLING STONES RECORDS / JOHN PASCHE / 1970

ROLLING STONES / *FORTY LICKS* / VIRGIN RECORDS / JOHN PASCHE / TOM HINGSTON STUDIO / 2002

GRATEFUL DEAD / BOB THOMAS & OWSLEY STANLEY / 1969

Owsley Stanley (a.k.a. "Bear"), LSD supplier on a massive scale and sound man for the Grateful Dead in their late-'60s heyday, was tired of confusing the Dead's and other bands' stage equipment at festivals and decided that a distinctive marking on the Dead's gear would make things easier. The inspiration for his "Steal Your Face" design came from a white-orange-and-blue circular design he saw while driving on a California freeway. Stanley thought the general shape with an added lightning bolt cutting across it would be an easily recognizable symbol and mentioned the idea to graphic-artist friend Bob Thomas, who was then working at the band's warehouse (and who would later create the *Live/Dead* and *Bear's Choice* album covers). After Thomas sketched out the concept, another friend, Ernie Fischbach, made a stencil and spray-painted the mark on an amp. Later, Stanley thought of adding the skull and Thomas created the now-iconic final version.

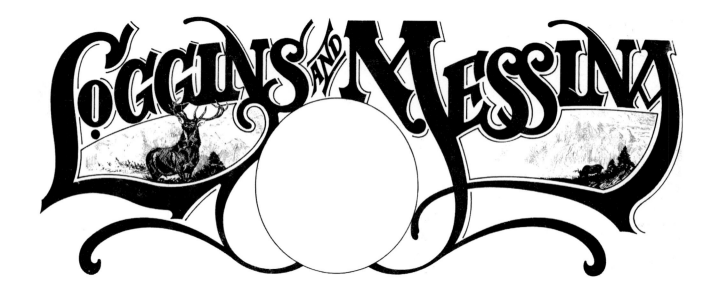

NEIL YOUNG / *HARVEST* / REPRISE RECORDS / TOM WILKES / 1972

# THE BEATLES

THE BEATLES / IVOR ARBITER & EDDIE STOKES / 1963

The Fab Four's "drop-T" logo was born in London's Drum City music shop when Ringo Starr and Beatles manager Brian Epstein went to buy Starr a Ludwig drum set. It was April 1963, almost a year before the band's celebrated trip to the United States, and Epstein sought to advertise the mop-topped icons with their name painted large enough across the front skin to overshadow Ludwig's copyright mark. Drum City owner Ivor Arbiter evidently sketched a few rough logo ideas, one of which contained the subterranean-T concept. Epstein and Starr liked what they saw, so Arbiter went to fetch a sign painter located nearby named Eddie Stokes who applied the design. On May 12, 1963, Ringo premiered his new Beatles-branded Ludwig set for the British TV show *Thank Your Lucky Stars*.

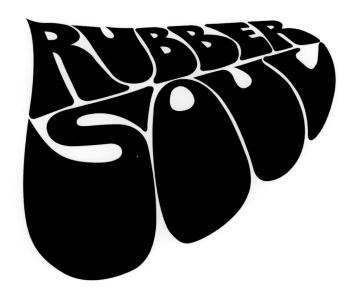

THE BEATLES / *A HARD DAYS NIGHT* MOVIE LOGO / UNITED ARTISTS / 1964

THE BEATLES / *RUBBER SOUL* / CAPITOL RECORDS / CHARLES FRONT / 1965

PAUL MCCARTNEY / *CHAOS AND CREATION IN THE BACKYARD* / EMI RECORDS / STYLOROUGE / 2005

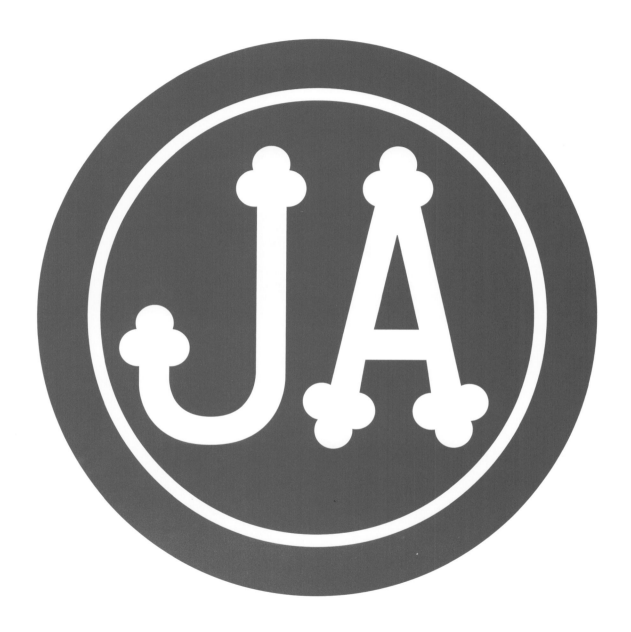

JEFFERSON AIRPLANE / *BARK* / GRUNT RECORDS / 1971

# JEFFERSON STARSHIP

JEFFERSON STARSHIP  /  *RED OCTOPUS*  /  GRUNT RECORDS  /  GRIBBITT!  /  1975

# STARSHIP

STARSHIP  /  *KNEE DEEP IN THE HOOPLA*  /  GRUNT RECORDS  /  TED RAESS  /  1985

REO SPEEDWAGON / EPIC RECORDS / 1971

ELECTRIC LIGHT ORCHESTRA / UNITED ARTISTS RECORDS / KOSH / 1976

JOURNEY

ESC4P3

JOURNEY / *ESCAPE* / COLUMBIA RECORDS / JIM WELCH / 1991

# EMERSON , LAKE & POWELL

EMERSON, LAKE & POWELL / POLYGRAM RECORDS / DEBRA ANNE BISHOP / 1975

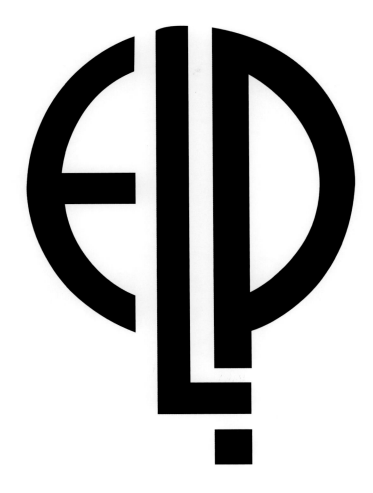

EMERSON, LAKE & PALMER / MANTICORE RECORDS / H.R. GIGER / 1973

Swiss surrealist artist H.R. Giger created this monogram design in 1973 for Emerson, Lake & Palmer's fifth studio album, originally called *Whip Some Skull on Ya* and officially renamed *Brain Salad Surgery* (both titles supposedly being obscure references to oral sex). The logo was extremely popular in the mid-to-late 1970s and has remained in use by the band for more than 30 years. Giger is perhaps best known for his Oscar-winning visual designs for the 1979 science-fiction classic *Alien*.

ORLEANS / MCA RECORDS / MARILYN MASON / 1980

ORLEANS / ABC RECORDS / 1973

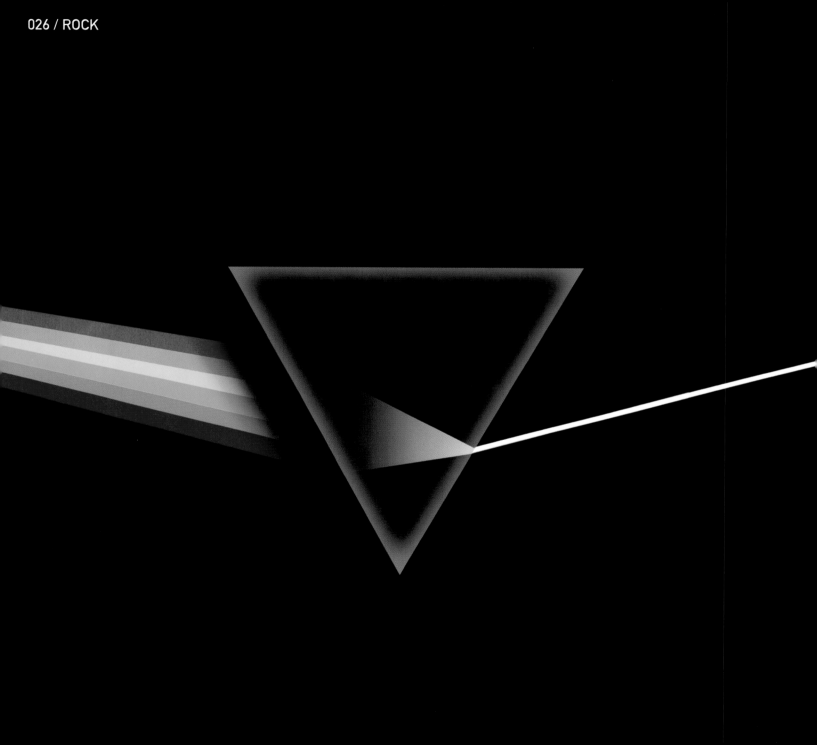

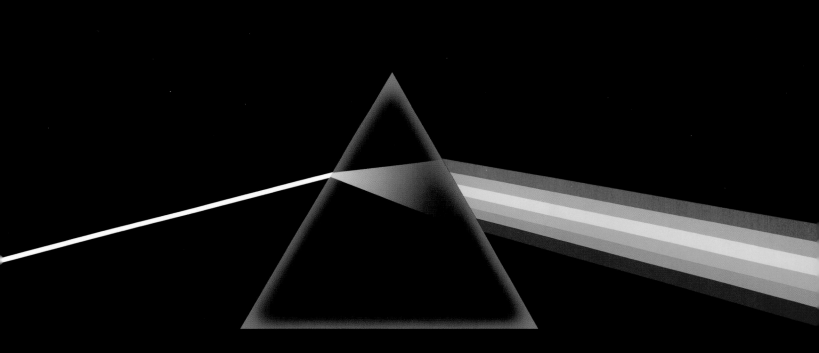

PINK FLOYD / *DARK SIDE OF THE MOON* / CAPITOL RECORDS / HIPGNOSIS / 1973

MOLLY HATCHET / EPIC RECORDS / FRANK FRAZETTA / 1978

38 SPECIAL / *SPECIAL FORCES* / A&M RECORDS / PHILIP GIPS / 1982

DEEP PURPLE / *PERFECT STRANGERS* / MERCURY RECORDS / CRAIG SPROVACH / 1984

LED ZEPPELIN / *LED ZEPPELIN IV* / ATLANTIC RECORDS / 1971

*Led Zeppelin IV*'s cover art featured a quartet of obscure symbols (sometimes referred to as runes or sigils) that were chosen by the band members to represent themselves. For Jimmy Page, the "ZoSo" alluded to ancient astrological, alchemical, and occultist references to Saturn, Mercury, and the writings of Aleister Crowley. Second in the series, John Paul Jones' design of a circle with three overlapping ellipses is a rune said to symbolize competency and confidence. Next is John Bonham's trio of interlocking rings that resemble a drum set viewed from above but also signify the Christian Trinity or possibly the trinity of man, woman, and child. (It also appeared on the label of one of Bonzo's favorite beers.) Lastly, Robert Plant's icon is that of Ma'at, an Egyptian feather representing truth, justice, and writing.

THIN LIZZY / MERCURY RECORDS / JIM FITZPATRICK / 1976

The who

THE WHO / MCA RECORDS / BRIAN PIKE / 1964

AEROSMITH / *ROCKS* / COLUMBIA RECORDS / RAY TABANO / 1976

AEROSMITH / *GET YOUR WINGS* / COLUMBIA RECORDS / RAY TABANO / 1974

AEROSMITH / *PERMANENT VACATION* / GEFFEN RECORDS / RAY TABANO / 1987

STRAY CATS / *BUILT FOR SPEED* / EMI AMERICA / 1982

THE KINKS / COMPLEAT RECORDS / 1984

SCANDAL / *WARRIOR* / COLUMBIA RECORDS / GEORGINA LEHNER / 1984

DIVINYLS / *WHAT A LIFE!* / CHRYSALIS RECORDS / 1985

DIVINYLS / VIRGIN RECORDS / INGE SCHAPP / 1991

RUSH / MERCURY RECORDS / PAUL WELDON / 1974

OASIS / CREATION RECORDS / BRIAN CANNON / 1994

OASIS / *STANDING ON THE SHOULDERS OF GIANTS* / EPIC RECORDS / GEM ARCHER / 2000

BLIND FAITH / PATCO RECORDS / 1969

JACKSON BROWNE / *THE PRETENDER* / ASYLUM RECORDS / GARY BURDEN / 1976

# LOU REED

LOU REED / *TRANSFORMER* / RCA RECORDS / ERNST THORMAHLEN / 1972

# THE DOORS

THE DOORS / ELEKTRA RECORDS / WILLIAM S HARVEY / 1967

# NEON HORSE

NEON HORSE / TOOTH & NAIL RECORDS / INVISIBLE CREATURE / 2006

THE WILDBIRDS / PAT'S RECORD COMPANY / CHRIS BILHEIMER / 2006

FLEETWOOD MAC / *RUMOURS* / WARNER BROS. RECORDS / LARRY VIGNON / 1977

THE LONELY HEARTS / TOOTH & NAIL RECORDS / INVISIBLE CREATURE / 2006

SANTANA / *ABRAXAS* / COLUMBIA RECORDS / BOB VENOSA / 1970

# OH YES

The classic logo that fans immediately associate with Yes was actually the third incarnation of the band's branding. First came guitarist Peter Banks' straightforward design for the 1969 debut album. Three years and three albums later, prolific artist/architect Roger Dean tried his hand at the task for the band's fourth album, *Fragile*. Dissatisfied with his first effort, Dean gave it another go for *Close to the Edge,* and his new logo set the gold standard for '70s rock iconography. The oozing curves, deft strokes, 3-D feel, the "y" and "s" snaking through the "e"—all of this Dean painstakingly managed by hand without the modern aid of computers.

His influences of art nouveau and psychedelia are readily apparent and reappear in Dean's later design work, most notably for the prog-rock supergroup Asia. Except for a brief stint in the mid-1980s beginning with the group's *90125* album—when it was retired in favor of Garry Mouat's yellow, magenta, and blue circle-Y design—and for Peter Max's colorful rendering on 1996's *Talk*, Dean's logo has been the graphic face of Yes throughout the band's career. The original logo artwork has even graced the walls of London's prestigious Victoria & Albert Museum.

YES / ATLANTIC RECORDS / ROGER DEAN / 1972

CHICAGO / *HOT STREETS* / COLUMBIA RECORDS / NICK FASCIANO / 1970

Few bands gave more attention to their logo than the prolific chart-toppers Chicago. Nick Fasciano's silhouetted script design became the centerpiece of nearly every album cover in the band's discography, from *Chicago II* in 1970 (after the jazzy ensemble abridged its name from the initial record's Chicago Transit Authority) up through *Chicago XXX* in 2006. Columbia Records art director John Berg was an early driving force in defining Chicago's image. Berg incorporated the signature typography into creative layouts that resembled leather, wood, gold, and even chocolate. James Pankow, Terry Kath, Peter Cetera, and company were rarely pictured on the cover; the logo spoke for itself . . . and still does. Throughout Chicago's many transformations in style and lineup over the years, Fasciano's typographic icon has stood the test of time as a mainstay of the band's popularity and success.

TRIUMPH / TML ENTERTAINMENT / 1979

UFO / *OBSESSION* / CHRYSALIS RECORDS / 1978

ZEBRA / ATLANTIC RECORDS / 1983

APRIL WINE / *FIRST GLANCE* / CAPITOL RECORDS / BOB LEMM / 1978

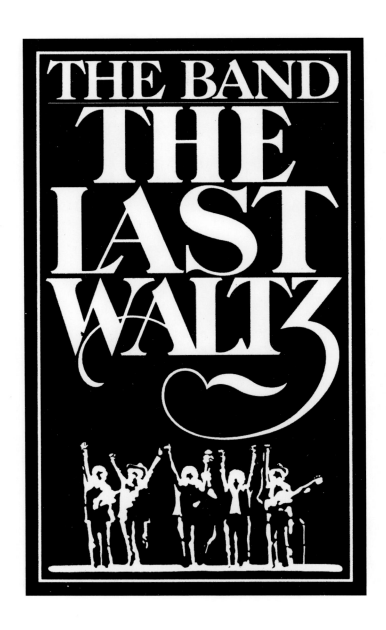

# U2
# W
# A
# R

THE BAND / *THE LAST WALTZ* / WARNER BROS. RECORDS / CASADO LTD. / 1978

U2 / *WAR* / ISLAND RECORDS / 1983

CHEAP TRICK / EPIC RECORDS / PAULA SCHER / 1971

TOTO / *TURN BACK* / COLUMBIA RECORDS / TONY LANE / 1981

ASIA / GEFFEN RECORDS / ROGER DEAN / 1982

THE FIRM / ATLANTIC RECORDS / STEVE MAHER / 1985

# BRUCE SPRINGSTEEN

BRUCE SPRINGSTEEN / *BORN TO RUN* / COLUMBIA RECORDS / JOHN BERG & ANDY ENGEL / 1975

*Bruce Springsteen*

BRUCE SPRINGSTEEN / *GREETINGS FROM ASBURY PARK, N.J.* / COLUMBIA RECORDS / 1973

# PRETENDERS

THE PRETENDERS / SIRE RECORDS / KEVIN HUGHES / 1980

QUEEN / EMI RECORDS / FREDDIE MERCURY / 1973

Using his art-college background in illustration and graphic design, Freddie Mercury created the Queen crest in advance of the group's self-titled debut release. He based the iconography on the signs of the Zodiac—fairies for Virgo (Freddie Mercury), a crab for Cancer (Brian May), lions for Leo (John Deacon and Roger Taylor)—and added the mythic symbol of a rising phoenix. What began as Mercury's simple sketch for the back of the 1973 *Queen* album cover evolved into the more detailed and sophisticated design seen here.

*Quicksilver Messenger Service*

QUICKSILVER MESSENGER SERVICE / *SOLID SILVER* / EDSEL RECORDS / ROY KOHARA / 1975

*Bob Seger & The Silver Bullet Band*

BOB SEGER & THE SILVER BULLET BAND / *AGAINST THE WIND* / CAPITOL RECORDS / ROY KOHARA / 1980

GIN BLOSSOMS / *OUTSIDE LOOKING IN* / INTERSCOPE RECORDS / T42DESIGN / 1999

JIMI HENDRIX / *THE ULTIMATE EXPERIENCE* / MCA RECORDS / STYLOROUGE / 1993

KENNY LOGGINS / *CELEBRATE ME HOME* / COLUMBIA RECORDS / MARTIN DONALD / 1977

PAT BENATAR / *CRIMES OF PASSION* / CHRYSALIS RECORDS / 1980

HEART / *DREAMBOAT ANNIE* / MUSHROOM RECORDS / JIM RIMMER / 1976

# THE POLICE
# THE POLICE

THE POLICE / *SYNCHRONICITY* / A&M RECORDS / JEFF AYEROFF & NORMAN MOORE / 1983

# THE POLICE

THE POLICE / *REGGATTA DE BLANC* / A&M RECORDS / MICHAEL ROSS / 1979

THE ALARM / *STRENGTH* / IRS RECORDS / 1985

THE ALARM / *DECLARATION* / IRS RECORDS / MICHAEL ROSS / 1984

THE ALARM / IRS RECORDS / 1983

10CC / UK RECORDS / 1973

ZZ TOP / *ELIMINATOR* / WARNER BROS. RECORDS / BOB ALFORD / 1983

LIVING COLOUR / EPIC RECORDS / 1988

TONIC / *SUGAR* / UNIVERSAL RECORDS / SMOG DESIGN / JERI HEIDEN / 1999

# Rainbow

RAINBOW / POLYDOR RECORDS / FIN COSTELLO / 1976

DEEP PURPLE / *STORMBRINGER* / EMI RECORDS / 1974

DERRINGER / *SWEET EVIL* / BLUE SKY RECORDS / 1977

THE RASMUS  /  PLAYGROUND MUSIC  /  HENRIK WALSE  /  2003

BLUE ÖYSTER CULT / *ON YOUR FEET OR ON YOUR KNEES* / CBS RECORDS / GERARD HUERTA / 1975

TED NUGENT / *CAT SCRATCH FEVER* / EPIC RECORDS / GERARD HUERTA / 1977

# INTERVIEW WITH GERARD HUERTA

Huerta was educated at the Art Center College of Design and began his professional career in 1974 as an album cover designer with CBS Records in New York. He left CBS in 1976 to start Gerard Huerta Design, Inc. and has been drawing letters and numbers ever since. He can be credited with some of the most iconic logos in the world, including Swiss Army Brands, Waldenbooks, Ringling Bros. and Barnum & Bailey Circus, Nabisco, Calvin Klein's Eternity, and Arista Records. He also created the mastheads of *Time, Money, People, The Atlantic Monthly, PC Magazine, Adweek, Us, Conde Nast Traveler,* and *Architectural Digest.*

• You designed some of the most iconic rock logos to come out of the 1970s. The AC/DC logo has become not just one of the most recognizable music logos, but one of the world's most identifiable logos in general. Can you give us the story behind it?

This was the second piece of lettering I did for the band's album covers. The first was *High Voltage* which showed a different configuration of AC/DC and some lightning bolt–style lettering. The second album lettering, which you are referring to, was done for one called *Let There Be Rock.* The cover showed the band on stage with a light beam coming from the sky. The influence was Gutenberg's Bible type with a twist: in color and dimensional. I had used this style two years before with an album called *On Your Feet or On Your Knees* by Blue Öyster Cult. That live album was really the source.

• Are you still proud every time you see someone wearing that logo on a T-shirt (I personally see someone wearing it almost every day), or, after 30 years, are you over it?

I don't know if "proud" is right. Logos are nothing without exposure and these four letters have had a lot of that. This lettering is one of so many pieces of artwork I have produced. There was nothing special about creating album art back then for me, as it was what I did each and every day. But I recall something that Christopher Walken said in the famous *SNL* cowbell skit: "You just never know what's gonna click."

• Do you mind if I ask how much you originally got paid for it?

I was paid for one album art cover use as shown in the purchase order. That is all I can tell you.

• It's also one of the most copied logos in the world. Is that flattering?

Well, it happens to be one of the easiest to copy. I don't think I have ever created another piece of art that was made entirely of straight lines.

• So how do you feel about designers like yourself getting paid for usage rights now? As professionals, it seems like we should really make sure to build things like that into our contracts when doing work like this. I mean, it's got to be a thorn in your side knowing how much money people have made off putting your logo on T-shirts, posters, and stickers.

One must protect oneself. I have drawers full of contracts. But my experience is the better the artist, the worse the businessman. Great artwork is difficult to produce if money is the primary motivation.

• You've also done great logos for Ted Nugent, Blue Öyster Cult, Boston, and Foreigner. How did you get involved with doing design for music, and get to work with these classic bands?

My first job out of art school was as an album designer with CBS in New York. I was highly influenced by the Los Angeles music scene when I was in school and I was fortunate to work with great art directors like John Berg and Bob Defrin in New York.

AC/DC / ATLANTIC RECORDS / GERARD HUERTA / 1977

• Now this was the '70s, so you were doing everything by hand. What was it like? Was it a nightmare doing revisions and showing the bands color options?

I was educated to leave school with a trade. I learned how to draw, letter, and understand good typography. I was also good with paint and ink and all of the materials we used to create reproducible artwork. It did take longer and I am thankful for my Mac. But as I said earlier, it was just what I did and was expected to do. You showed a portfolio of work and produced that level or better every time you were (and are) hired. There were fewer changes then because the people you worked for were more on your level and could understand a sketch, as they themselves could draw. The computer is very democratic, therefore you never know how educated the person is that you are working for anymore. This is why there are more changes now: people don't draw anymore and never develop an ability to see as a result.

• Who were your favorite bands to work with?

I was actually really insulated from the bands. The assignments always came from the creative directors at the record companies, which allowed me more freedom to experiment. Also, at the time the artwork was created, most of the bands were relatively new and without much clout.

• The AC/DC logo being such a classic, which other rock logos do you put in the same league with it?

I think there are many, many works that are great, and it would be tough for me to single out just a few.

FOREIGNER / ATLANTIC RECORDS / GERARD HUERTA / 1976

BOSTON  /  EPIC RECORDS  /  GERARD HUERTA  /  1976

VAN HALEN / WARNER BROS. RECORDS / DAVID LEE ROTH & DAVE BHANG / 1978

VAN HALEN / *VAN HALEN II* / WARNER BROS. RECORDS / 1979

VAN HALEN / *FOR UNLAWFUL CARNAL KNOWLEDGE* / WARNER BROS. RECORDS / 1991

# matchbox 20

MATCHBOX 20 / *YOURSELF OR SOMEONE LIKE YOU* / ATLANTIC RECORDS / VALERIE WAGNER / 1996

LOCAL H / *AS GOOD AS DEAD* / ISLAND RECORDS / 1996

KANSAS / *BEST OF* / CBS ASSOCIATED RECORDS / 1984

SAMMY HAGAR / *STREET MACHINE* / CAPITOL RECORDS / BOB BUHL / 1979

MARILLION / EMI RECORDS / 1983

SURVIVOR / *VITAL SIGNS* / VOLCANO RECORDS / 1981

MICHELLE SHOCKED / MERCURY RECORDS / 1988

QUARTERFLASH / GEFFEN RECORDS / TOMMY STEELE & CHRIS WHORF / 1981

THE ROMANTICS / NEMPEROR RECORDS / 1980

VELVET REVOLVER / RCA RECORDS / BRETT KILROE & ROBIN C. HENDRICKSON / 2004

INXS / X / ATLANTIC RECORDS / NICK EGAN & TOM BOUMAN / 1990

VELVET REVOLVER / RCA RECORDS / BRETT KILROE & ROBIN C. HENDRICKSON / 2004

EVE 6 / RCA RECORDS / BRETT KILROE / 1998

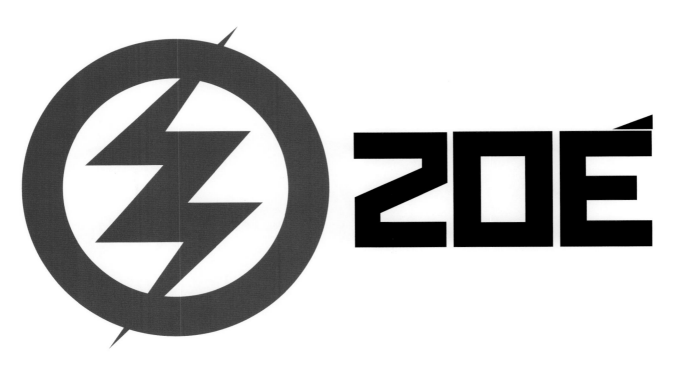

INXS / *SWITCH* / EPIC RECORDS / BRANDY FLOWER / 2005

ZOÉ / *THE ROOM* EP / NOISELAB RECORDS / 2005

# BLACK REBEL MOTORCYCLE CLUB

BLACK REBEL MOTORCYCLE CLUB / *HOWL* / RCA RECORDS / MIKE PROSENKO / 2005

MC5 / ELEKTRA RECORDS / GARY GRIMSHAW / 1969

THUNDER EXPRESS / *WE PLAY FOR PLEASURE* / DEAF & DUMB RECORDS / HENRIK WALSE / 2005

THE HELLACOPTERS / *ROCK & ROLL IS DEAD.* / LIQUOR & POKER RECORDS / HENRIK WALSE / 2007

SINCE 1994

The Hellacopters

HIGH ENERGY ROCK'N'ROLL

THE HELLACOPTERS  /  T-SHIRT LOGO  /  HENRIK WALSE  /  2003

LAVAHEAD / *ANYONE BUT ME* / KARLSSONWILKER / 1997

THE BROUGHT LOW / *KINGS FROM QUEENS* / TEE PEE RECORDS / MORNING BREATH INC. / 2004

BOB SEGER & THE SILVER BULLET BAND / *STRANGER IN TOWN* / CAPITOL RECORDS / 1978

VERTICAL HORIZON / *EVERYTHING YOU WANT* / RCA RECORDS / SMOG DESIGN / JOHN HEIDEN / 1999

THE OUTLAWS  /  *OUTLAWS*  /  ARISTA RECORDS  /  ARTON ASSOC.  /  1975

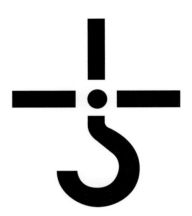

BLUE ÖYSTER CULT  /  CBS RECORDS  /  BILL GAWLIK  /  1972

TENACIOUS D  /  EPIC RECORDS  /  GREGG BERNSTEIN  /  2005

DAVE MATTHEWS BAND  /  DAVE MATTHEWS  /  1995

STYX / A&M RECORDS / CHUCK BEESON / 1974

BAD COMPANY / SWAN SONG RECORDS / BOB WYNNE / 1974

CHARLIE SEXTON / *PICTURES FOR PLEASURE* / MCA RECORDS / 1985

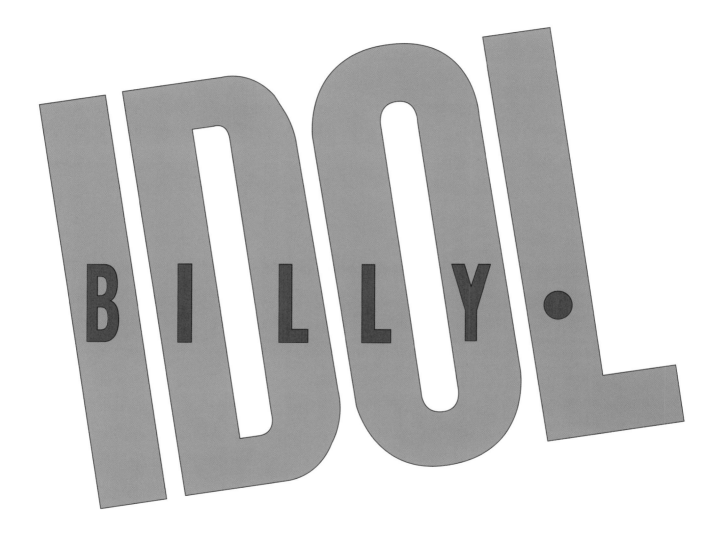

BILLY IDOL / CAPITOL RECORDS / JANET LEVINSON / 1983

A GHOST IS BORN TOUR '05

WILCO / A GHOST IS BORN TOUR LOGO / JASON MUNN / 2005

RINGSIDE / GEFFEN RECORDS / 2005

# squeeze

SQUEEZE / *BABYLON AND ON* / A&M RECORDS / STYLOROUGE / 1987

# THE BLASTERS

THE BLASTERS / WARNER BROS. RECORDS / 1981

# TED NUGENT

TED NUGENT / *FREE FOR ALL* / EPIC RECORDS / PAULA SCHER / 1976

BOXKAR / *COMIN' OUT SWINGIN* / 2006

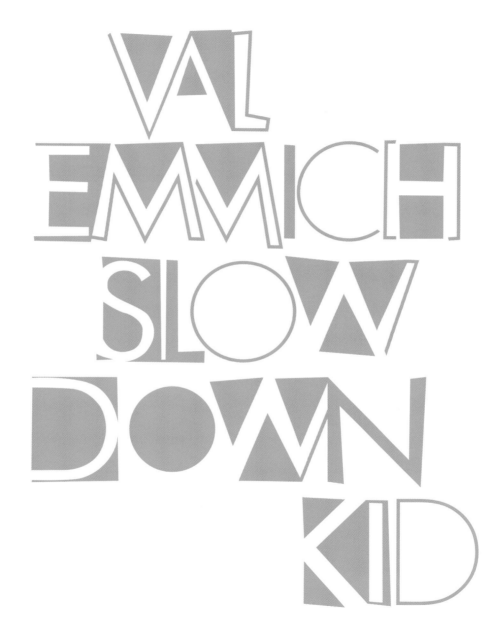

VAL EMMICH / *SLOW DOWN KID* / EPIC RECORDS / MORNING BREATH INC. / 2005

MARK JOSEPH / WARNER MUSIC GROUP / STYLOROUGE / 2004

# FOO FIGHTERS

FOO FIGHTERS  /  *ONE BY ONE*  /  RCA RECORDS  /  RAYMOND PETTIBON  /  2002

JAMESTOWN LTD.  /  *THE WORLD IS FALLING DOWN*  /  BODHI OSER  /  2006

# THE HIGHER

THE HIGHER  /  EPITAPH RECORDS  /  NICK PRITCHARD  /  2007

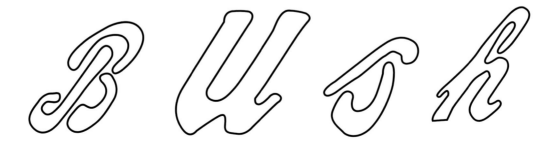

BUSH  /  *SIXTEEN STONE*  /  TRAUMA RECORDS  /  DAVID CARSON  /  1994

FOO FIGHTERS / *THE COLOUR AND THE SHAPE* / CAPITOL RECORDS / ANDY ENGEL / 1997

# ACE UP THEIR SLEEVE

When Ace Frehley joined KISS in 1973, he contributed more than just lead guitar—he also created the band's iconic logo. A former graphic designer, Frehley managed to synergize all the excitement and theatrics that defined KISS into a sleek red-and-yellow emblem with lightning bolts (soon to become a staple of heavy metal typography).

Interestingly, the lightning bolts drew fire in Germany because of their similarity with the insignia of the notorious Nazi SS combat force. As a result, KISS albums from Düsseldorf to Berlin always feature the bolts in reverse as "ZZ."

Thanks to brilliant marketing by the band (who emblazoned it on everything from KISS Kondoms™ to KISS Kaskets™), the KISS logo has become as pervasive and recognizable as the Rolling Stones' renowned tongue-and-lip design.

KISS  /  CASABLANCA RECORDS  /  ACE FREHLEY  /  1974

DIRTY LOOKS / *COOL FROM THE WIRE* / ATLANTIC RECORDS / BOB DEFRIN / 1987

BULLETBOYS / WARNER BROS. RECORDS / TED RAESS / 1988

SKID ROW / ATLANTIC RECORDS / BOB DEFRIN / 1989

GREAT WHITE / ENIGMA RECORDS / 1987

SAXON / CAROLINE RECORDS / 1979

EUROPE / HOT RECORDS / 1983

DEMON / CARRERE RECORDS / 1981

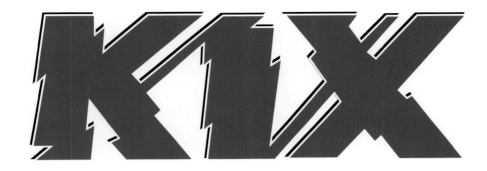

KIX / *MIDNIGHT DYNAMITE* / ATLANTIC RECORDS / 1985

POISON / ENIGMA RECORDS / 1986

CINDERELLA / *NIGHT SONGS* / MERCURY RECORDS / EMILY PEMBER / 1986

STRYPER / *TO HELL WITH THE DEVIL* / ENIGMA RECORDS / BRIAN AYUSO / 1986

FOZZY / PALM RECORDS / 2000

SPIÑAL TAP / *THIS IS SPIÑAL TAP* / SPIÑAL TAP PROD. / GREGORY BOONE / 1984

MAYDAY / *REVENGE* / A&M RECORDS / JOHN DISMUKES / 1982

LIZZY BORDEN / *GIVE 'EM THE AXE* / METAL BLADE RECORDS / VINCE GUTIERREZ / 1984

W.A.S.P. / *ANIMAL (FUCK LIKE A BEAST)* / MUSIC FOR NATIONS. / 1984

QUEENSRŸCHE / EMI RECORDS / TODD ROCKENFIELD / 1983

HELLOWEEN / NOISE RECORDS / PETER VAHLEFELD / 1985

KROKUS / *CHANGE OF ADDRESS* / ARISTA RECORDS / 1986

# TWISTED SISTER

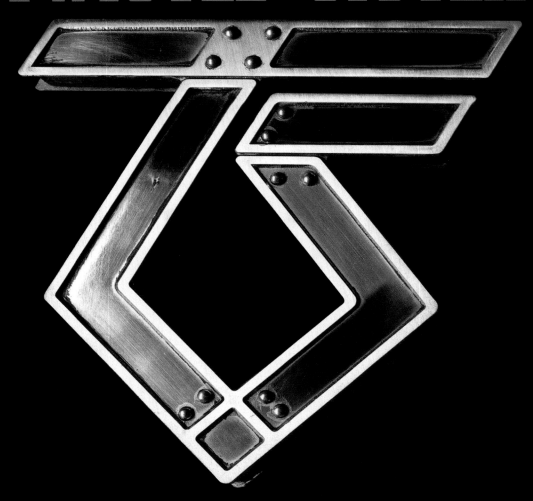

TWISTED SISTER  /  *YOU CAN'T STOP ROCK 'N' ROLL*  /  ATLANTIC RECORDS  /  1983

MÖTLEY CRÜE

MÖTLEY CRÜE / *TOO FAST FOR LOVE* / ELEKTRA RECORDS / 1981

MÖTLEY CRÜE / *DR. FEELGOOD* / ELEKTRA RECORDS / BOB DEFRIN / 1989

LOUDNESS  /  *LIGHTNING STRIKES*  /  SONY MUSIC ENTERTAINMENT (JAPAN)  /  1986

RATT / ATLANTIC RECORDS / 1983

QUIET RIOT / PASHA RECORDS / 1983

THE MICHAEL SCHENKER GROUP  /  CHRYSALIS RECORDS  /  1980

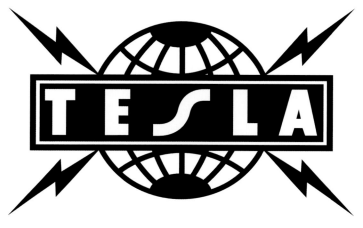

TESLA / GEFFEN RECORDS / 1986

NIGHT RANGER / *DAWN PATROL* / MCA RECORDS / JEFF LANCASTER / 1982

WHITE LION / *FIGHT TO SURVIVE* / ASYLUM RECORDS / 1985

QUEENSRŸCHE / *OPERATION: MINDCRIME* / EMI RECORDS / 1988

DOKKEN / ELEKTRA RECORDS / DAVE "THE KNAVE" WILLIAMS / 1982

DORO PESCH / WEA INTERNATIONAL / 1998

WHITESNAKE / UNITED ARTISTS RECORDS / 1979

OVERKILL / MEGAFORCE RECORDS / 1983

EXTREME / A&M RECORDS / 1989

GAMMA RAY / *LAND OF THE FREE* / NOISE INTERNATIONAL / EIKE GALL / 1995

BON JOVI / ISLAND RECORDS / 1985

EXTREME / *III SIDES TO EVERY STORY* / A&M RECORDS / LIZ VAP / 1992

PRETTY MAIDS / RED, HOT AND HEAVY / SONY RECORDS / 1984

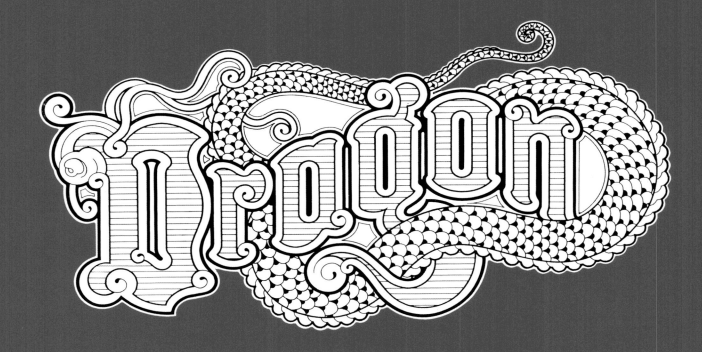

IRON MAIDEN / EMI RECORDS / STEVE HARRIS / 1980

ANNIHILATOR / ROADRUNNER RECORDS / LEN ROONEY / 1989

SCORPIONS / RCA RECORDS / 1975

TESTAMENT / ATLANTIC RECORDS / BILL BENSON / 1987

JUDAS PRIEST / CBS RECORDS / ROSLAV SZAYBO / 1978

THE DARKNESS / *PERMISSION TO LAND* / ATLANTIC RECORDS / 2003

DEF LEPPARD / *HIGH AND DRY* / MERCURY RECORDS / HIPGNOSIS / 1979

FASTWAY / COLUMBIA RECORDS / JO MIROWSKI / 1984

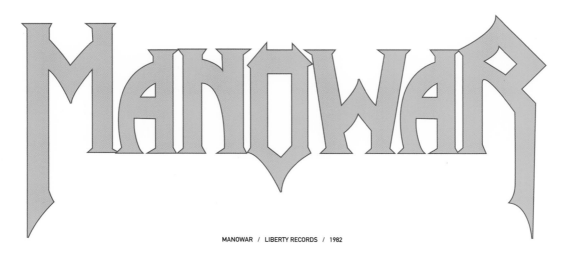

MANOWAR / LIBERTY RECORDS / 1982

OZZY OSBOURNE / *DOWN TO EARTH* / SONY RECORDS / 2001

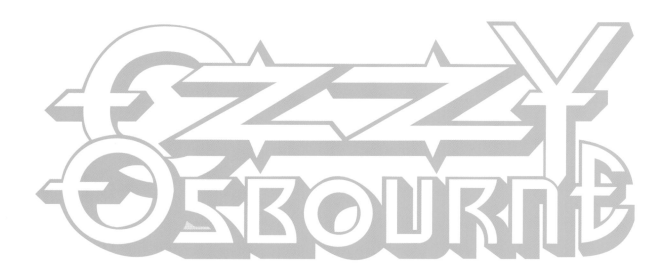

OZZY OSBOURNE / *NO MORE TEARS* / EPIC RECORDS / 1991

OZZY OSBOURNE / *DIARY OF A MADMAN* / JET RECORDS / 1981

# SOUNDGARDEN

SOUNDGARDEN / *LOUDER THAN LOVE* / A&M RECORDS / ART CHANTRY / 1989

# NASHVILLE PUSSY

NASHVILLE PUSSY / LOGO FOR CONCERT POSTER / ART CHANTRY / 2003

# SUPERSUCKERS

SUPERSUCKERS / SUB POP RECORDS / ART CHANTRY / 1990

CKY / *INFILTRATE•DESTROY•REBUILD* / ISLAND RECORDS / 2002

# INTERVIEW WITH T42DESIGN

Since launching t42design in 1997, Tom Jermann and Toby Yoo have done a lot of work for many of the music industry's heavies. Their killer portfolio is filled with a variety of work for a diverse group of artists including Alice Cooper, Def Leppard, Johnny Cash, KISS, Slayer, Slipknot, Willie Nelson, and Muddy Waters. They have created memorable logos for Slipknot, Gin Blossoms, Fear Factory, and Stone Sour, and most recently, Tom designed a landmark photography book of classic Van Halen images.

• Can we start with a little background information?

Well, I was born in Switzerland a few days before the '60s were over. Originally, I studied architecture and also worked in that field several years before moving to Pasadena in my mid-twenties to study graphic design at the Art Center College of Design. My first job was at MCA Records as a junior designer. This was the perfect place for me to get my feet wet and learn the ropes. I am a big music fan, and designing album covers and packagings is what I wanted to do. I also worked at Maverick Records before starting my own business.

• Was designing for music something you set out to focus on specifically?

Oh yes, music it was. Therefore coming to L.A. was the ideal playground—but a tough one at the same time. However, I believe that if you're passionate about something you will succeed . . . unless you actually do suck at what you are trying to do.

• You've worked with a lot of different genres of music. Is it harder for you to do a design you love for a band that you're just not into, or a style of music you don't really care for?

To work on a project that you just don't care for is hard, yet it is an unbelievable challenge to rise to. I feel that most of our results usually are based on the "vibe" we have with an artist—and then it doesn't matter whether it is Willie Nelson or Slayer or B.B. King.

• Off the top of your head, what would you say is the most famous band logo ever?

It must be KISS.

• Where do you look for inspiration and examples when working on a new logo design?

Actually everywhere else but music-related places. Let's just say "in the streets of Los Angeles." I find that this resource is quite inspiring . . .

• When you're working on a CD or logo design for a specific band, do you listen to their music over and over again during the process?

Definitely. Even if you know their music already, a new album may have a different theme or style that needs to be incorporated in the artwork or logo.

• Who have been your favorite bands or artists to work with?

The guys from Def Leppard have been fantastic. KISS are absolute pros, and loyal. And I have to say that Clown from Slipknot was amazing to work with—chaotic but very creative!

• Do you show a lot of options when you're doing a logo design? How often is the final logo that's chosen the one you would have picked?

We usually show three. Many designers make the mistake of showing options A, B, and C, with the latter being their least favorite. Of course the client picks C. We prefer to have all three options on the same level. That way I don't have a sleepless night with nightmares of the client walking around with a shirt of logo C on it! Also, if we are not happy with something, it literally does not leave the studio until we are happy, or the design gets canned altogether.

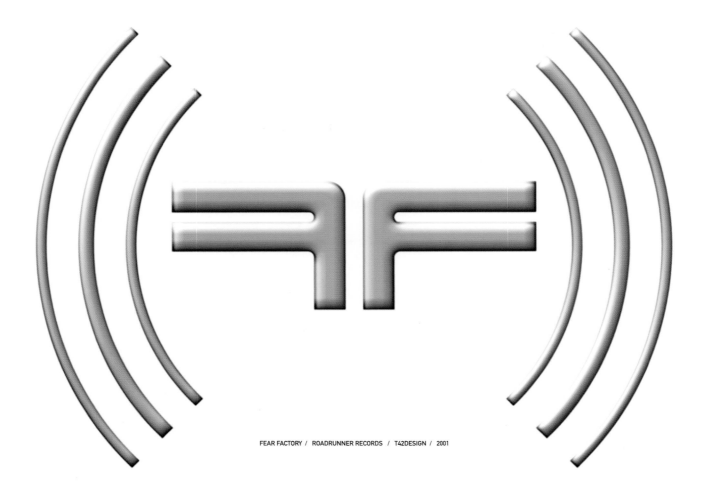

FEAR FACTORY / ROADRUNNER RECORDS / T42DESIGN / 2001

• What would you say are the five best band logos ever?

- **KISS**: So simple, but so powerful, and oh so controversial.

- The **Rolling Stones** tongue logo: How cool is that? It's just a mark, no words! Remarkable.

- The **Van Halen** "VH" logo: Just cool and classic.

- **AC/DC**: A great logo that lends itself well to being scratched into school desk tops, and just always looks great.

- **Chicago**: I love how they always incorporated their logo within the album art. No one else has really done that.

# SAOSIN

SAOSIN / CAPITOL RECORDS / 2003

CLUTCH / EARACHE RECORDS / 1992

PANTERA / ELEKTRA RECORDS / BOB DEFRIN / 1990

DANZIG

DEATH ANGEL / ENIGMA RECORDS / 1987

BLACK SABBATH / WARNER BROS. RECORDS / 1970

BLACK SABBATH / WARNER BROS. RECORDS / 1970

BLACK SABBATH / *MASTER OF REALITY* / WARNER BROS. RECORDS / BLOOMSBURY GROUP / 1971

# BLACK SABBATH

BLACK SABBATH / *FORBIDDEN* / EMI RECORDS / 1995

# Black Sabbath

BLACK SABBATH / *BLACK SABBATH, VOL. 4* / WARNER BROS. RECORDS / BLOOMSBURY GROUP / 1972

WHITE ZOMBIE  /  GEFFEN RECORDS  /  ROB ZOMBIE  /  1992

FIGHT / *WAR OF WORDS* / EPIC RECORDS / 1993

VALIENT THORR / VOLCOM ENTERTAINMENT / RYAN IMMEGART / 2005

ANTHRAX / MEGAFORCE RECORDS / 1984

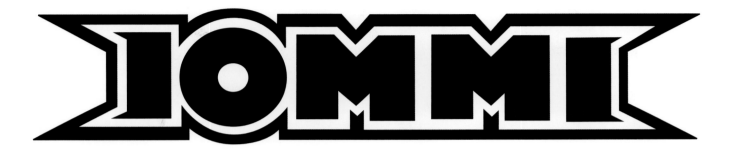

IOMMI / DIVINE RECORDS / 2000

NUCLEAR ASSAULT / COMBAT RECORDS / 1986

METALLICA / MEGAFORCE RECORDS / JAMES HETFIELD / 1983

MEGADETH / COMBAT RECORDS / 1985

MOTÖRHEAD / CHISWICK RECORDS / JOE PETAGNO / 1977

WHITE ZOMBIE / *LA SEXORCISTO: DEVIL MUSIC VOL. 1* / GEFFEN RECORDS / ROB ZOMBIE / 1992

KORN / EPIC RECORDS / 1993

ALICE IN CHAINS / COLUMBIA RECORDS / DAVID COLEMAN / 1990

STONE SOUR / ROADRUNNER RECORDS / T42DESIGN / 2002

AUDIOSLAVE / SONY RECORDS / PETER CURZON / 2002

SALIVA / *EVERY SIX SECONDS* / ISLAND RECORDS / MORNING BREATH INC. / 2000

# PARADISE LOST

PARADISE LOST / *ICON* / MUSIC FOR NATIONS / STYLOROUGE / 1993

# PAPA ROACH

PAPA ROACH / DREAMWORKS RECORDS / P.R. BROWN / 2000

12 STONES / WIND-UP RECORDS / 2002

EIGHTEEN VISIONS / SONY RECORDS / P.R. BROWN / 2006

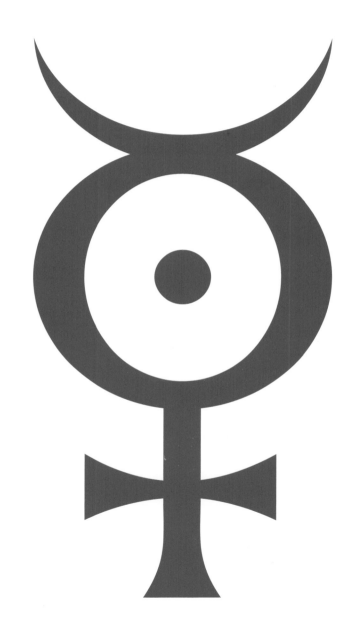

MARILYN MANSON / *HOLY WOOD* / NOTHING RECORDS / P.R. BROWN / 2000

POWERMAN 5000

POWERMAN 5000  /  *TRANSFORM*  /  DREAMWORKS RECORDS  /  2003

HELMET

HELMET  /  *MEANTIME*  /  INTERSCOPE RECORDS  /  1992

nonpoint

NONPOINT  /  MCA RECORDS  /  2000

RAMMSTEIN / MOTOR MUSIC / DIRK RUDOLPH / 1995

FILTER / *TITLE OF RECORD* / REPRISE RECORDS / DEBORAH NORCROSS / 1999

# WOLFMOTHER

WOLFMOTHER / MODULAR RECORDINGS / MYLES HESKETT / 2004

# TOTIMOSHI

TOTIMOSHI / *LADRON* / VOLCOM ENTERTAINMENT / 2006

# SYSTEM OF A DOWN

SYSTEM OF A DOWN / *TOXICITY* / COLUMBIA RECORDS / BRANDY FLOWER / 2001

KAMELOT / NOISE RECORDS / 1995

# FIGHT PARIS

FIGHT PARIS / TRUSTKILL RECORDS / 2003

# DAMAGEPLAN

DAMAGEPLAN / *NEW FOUND POWER* / ELEKTRA RECORDS / MARK O. / 2004

VANNA / *THE SEARCH PARTY THAT NEVER CAME* / EPITAPH RECORDS / 2006

ANOTHER BREATH / *NOT NOW, NOT EVER* / RIVALRY RECORDS / 2004

YEAR LONG DISASTER  /  VOLCOM ENTERTAINMENT  /  2007

MEMPHIS MAY FIRE / TRUSTKILL RECORDS / 2007

# COHEED AND CAMBRIA

COHEED AND CAMBRIA / *IN KEEPING SECRETS OF SILENT EARTH: 3* / EQUAL VISION RECORDS / BILL SCOVILLE / 2003

DEATH BEFORE DISCO / GOOD LIFE RECORDINGS / 2004

TERROR / TRUSTKILL RECORDS / 2003

TIME FOR LIVING

TIME FOR LIVING / RIVALRY RECORDS / 2005

DEFTONES / *WHITE PONY* / MAVERICK RECORDS / 2000

RAGE AGAINST THE MACHINE / *RENEGADES* / EPIC RECORDS / 2000

L7 / *BRICKS ARE HEAVY* / SLASH RECORDS / RANDALL MARTIN / 1992

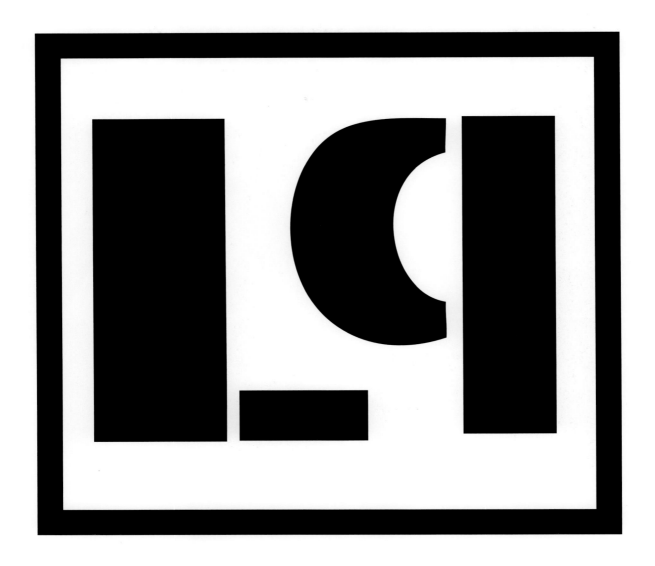

LINKIN PARK / WARNER BROS. RECORDS / 2000

LINKIN PARK / *HYBRID THEORY* / WARNER BROS. RECORDS / FRANK MADDOCKS / 2000

LINKIN PARK / *LIVE IN TEXAS* / WARNER BROS. RECORDS / FLEM / 2003

LINKIN PARK / *MINUTES TO MIDNIGHT* / WARNER BROS. RECORDS / FRANK MADDOCKS / 2007

LIMP BIZKIT / *SIGNIFICANT OTHER* / INTERSCOPE RECORDS / 1999

LIMP BIZKIT / INTERSCOPE RECORDS / 2001

LIMP BIZKIT / INTERSCOPE RECORDS / 2005

AFI / *DECEMBERUNDERGROUND* / INTERSCOPE RECORDS / MORNING BREATH INC. / 2006

AFI / *SING THE SORROW* / INTERSCOPE RECORDS / MORNING BREATH INC. / 2003

ASG / *FEELIN' GOOD IS GOOD ENOUGH* / VOLCOM ENTERTAINMENT / 2005

RAGING SPEEDHORN / *FUCK THE VOODOOMAN* / ZTT RECORDS / STYLOROUGE / 2002

ILL NIÑO / *ONE NATION UNDERGROUND* / ROADRUNNER RECORDS / CHARLES DOOHER / 2005

KANDI CODED / *TIME WASTED IS NOT WASTED TIME* / VOLCOM ENTERTAINMENT / 2006

EVANESCENCE / WIND-UP RECORDS / 2000

BULLET FOR MY VALENTINE / TRUSTKILL RECORDS / LA BOCA LTD. / 2004

THUNDERSTONE / NUCLEAR BLAST RECORDS / 2003

AND THE HERO FAILS / *EMPIRE SMILE* / 2005

APOCALYPTICA / UNIVERSAL RECORDS / 1998

DROWNING POOL / *SINNER* / WIND-UP RECORDS / 2001

GODSMACK / REPUBLIC RECORDS / BAUDA DESIGN LAB / 1998

40 BELOW SUMMER / LONDON-SIRE RECORDS / T42 DESIGN / 2001

DISTURBED / *BELIEVE* / REPRISE RECORDS / MICK HAGGERTY / 2002

HIM / VILLE HERMANNI VALO / 1996

# QUEENS OF THE STONE AGE

QUEENS OF THE STONE AGE / *SONGS FOR THE DEAF* / INTERSCOPE RECORDS / 2002

QUEENS OF THE STONE AGE / *ERA VULGARIS* / INTERSCOPE RECORDS / MORNING BREATH INC. / 2007

A PERFECT CIRCLE / VIRGIN RECORDS / MAYNARD JAMES KEENAN / 2000

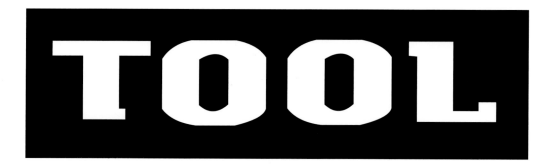

TOOL / *UNDERTOW* / ZOO ENTERTAINMENT / ADAM JONES / 1996

TOOL / *LATERALUS* / ZOO ENTERTAINMENT / ADAM JONES / 2001

TOOL / *10,000 DAYS* / ZOO ENTERTAINMENT / ADAM JONES / 2006

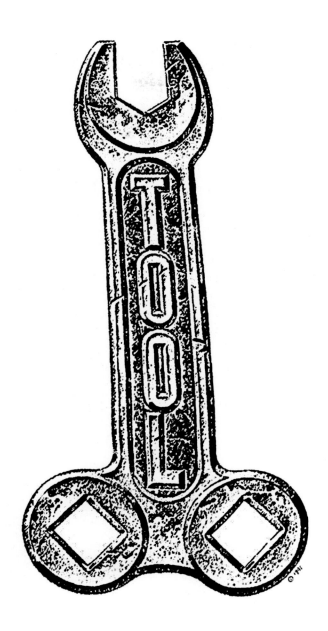

TOOL / CAM DE LEON / 1995

MY DYING BRIDE / PEACEVILLE RECORDS / 1993

DEICIDE / ROADRUNNER RECORDS / 1990

MORGUL / SPV RECORDS / 1997

MALIGNANCY / UNITED GUTTURAL RECORDS / 1993

MOONSPELL / CENTURY MEDIA / 1995

CANNIBAL CORPSE / METAL BLADE RECORDS / 1990

OBITUARY / ROADRUNNER RECORDS / ROB MAYWORTH / 1989

VENOM / COMBAT RECORDS / 1981

# DIMMU BORGIR

DIMMU BORGIR / *ENTHRONE DARKNESS TRIUMPHANT* / NUCLEAR BLAST RECORDS / P. GRØN / 1997

DIMMU BORGIR  /  *FOR ALL TID*  /  NUCLEAR BLAST RECORDS  /  1994

MORBID ANGEL / EARACHE RECORDS / 1989

DARKTHRONE / PEACEVILLE RECORDS / 1991

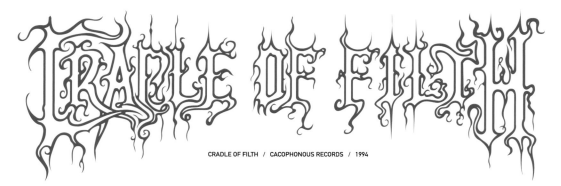

CRADLE OF FILTH / CACOPHONOUS RECORDS / 1994

BLEEDING THROUGH / TRUSTKILL RECORDS / INVISIBLE CREATURE / 2003

HATEBREED / SMORGASBORD RECORDS / 1996

PUNGENT STENCH  /  NUCLEAR BLAST RECORDS  /  1989

BLEEDING THROUGH / *THE TRUTH* / TRUSTKILL RECORDS / INVISIBLE CREATURE / 2006

# TRAPT

TRAPT / *SOMEONE IN CONTROL* / WARNER BROS. RECORDS / INVISIBLE CREATURE / 2005

# UNEARTH

UNEARTH / *III: IN THE EYES OF FIRE* / METAL BLADE RECORDS / INVISIBLE CREATURE / 2006

PROJECT 86 / TOOTH & NAIL RECORDS / INVISIBLE CREATURE / 2004

# INTERVIEW WITH DON CLARK OF INVISIBLE CREATURE

Founding members of the metal band Demon Hunter, the heavily tattooed, God-fearing, mama's-boy brothers Don and Ryan Clark also pour their creative passion and hearts into the twice-Grammy-nominated design work they do as Invisible Creature. Based in Seattle, the duo's client roster includes Korn, the Foo Fighters, and Chris Cornell, and they've designed logos for bands such as the All-American Rejects, Trapt, Unearth, and MxPx.

• You say you're self-taught. What does that mean? No design school training? No internships or design mentors?

As a child, I remember my answer to the famous question: "What do you want to be when you grow up?" My answer was always the same: "A major league baseball player or an artist." Apparently my position as first baseman for the Giants isn't going to become available anytime soon, so I've been running with option #2 for quite some time. Our grandfather, Al Paulsen, was an illustrator for NASA and an amazing inspiration while we were growing up. We just always wanted to be artists, and luckily we were pretty decent at it. In our teenage years and early twenties, we got heavily involved in music and the two passions just collided. We were basically designing during the day and playing clubs at night.

• How do you manage to balance your time between the design studio and the band?

Time management might be the best answer. When it comes to making a record, we devote our mornings to the writing process. For instance, our new record was written in large part during the hours of 7–9 A.M. For touring, we try and block out five weeks during the summer where we aren't taking much work. We started Demon Hunter five years ago, so it's been a juggling act for half a decade now. Four records and three tours under our belt, we are starting to get the hang of it.

• Do you have to do design work when you're on the road and touring sometimes?

We actually don't work on any projects while we are on the road. We literally shut down the studio while we are gone, but we make sure we have projects starting up as soon as we get back, so as to not skip a beat with clients.

• When you meet someone, and they ask what you do for a living, do you tell them you're a musician or a designer?

Actually, both. It really depends on who is asking, but typically my response is both.

• As far as design, how did you break into the music industry? Did you just build relationships with other musicians while you were touring, and that led to getting the work?

Ryan started a band called Focal Point in 1994 and quickly signed to Life Sentence Records that same year. I did their first 7-inch release and ended up doing quite a bit more work for Life Sentence. When Focal Point signed with Tooth & Nail Records in 1995, I ended up designing their album, which was my first album design, and Tooth & Nail seemed to dig my work, although I admit now I had no clue as to what I was doing. Before Demon Hunter, Ryan and I were in a band called Training For Utopia and we were on T&N

as well, so I guess you can say they definitely gave us our start. Instead of college, we were touring and meeting people in the industry. The rest, as they say, is history.

• Who have been your favorite bands to work with creatively?

Zao is a band that has always given us creative freedom. Bleeding Through, Throwdown . . . actually, quite a few bands are pretty lenient and are always cool with us just "doing our thing." Sometimes creative restrictions can be good—it gives us certain design parameters and that can be a positive thing—but mostly we love just pitching concepts and going for it. For Bleeding Through's album *The Truth*, we talked each band member into being covered in red dye and chocolate sauce for eight hours—and all in the name of art. Suckers.

• Who do you usually clash with more when creative differences arise, the bands or the labels?

Bands, for sure. Labels just usually want to please the band and move on with it.

• Do you design for other industries?

We have done a few projects outside the music world, and those are fun because they *aren't* music-related. It allows us to think outside the box sometimes. As much as we love doing non-music-related projects, the people that keep calling are involved in music. We aren't complaining—that is definitely our world.

• What are your personal Top 5 band logos of all-time?

Off the top of my head, I would say Metallica, AC/DC, Judas Priest, Van Halen, and HIM. Each is classic and genius in its own right.

DEMON HUNTER / SOLID STATE RECORDS / INVISIBLE CREATURE / 2004

THE SHOWDOWN / MONO VS STEREO / INVISIBLE CREATURE / 2005

THROWDOWN / TRUSTKILL RECORDS / INVISIBLE CREATURE / 2004

# THE CHARIOT

THE CHARIOT / *THE FIANCEE* / TOOTH & NAIL RECORDS / INVISIBLE CREATURE / 2007

TWELVE GAUGE VALENTINE / *SHOCK VALUE* / SOLID STATE RECORDS / INVISIBLE CREATURE / 2006

# SEPULTURA

SEPULTURA / *NATION* / ROADRUNNER RECORDS / 2001

SEPULTURA / ROADRUNNER RECORDS / 1999

# SEPULTURA

SEPULTURA / *CHAOS A.D.* / ROADRUNNER RECORDS / 1992

SLIPKNOT / T42DESIGN / 2004

SLIPKNOT / JOEY JORDISON / 1996

IRON MONKEY / EARACHE RECORDS / 1997

CHILDREN OF BODOM / NUCLEAR BLAST RECORDS / 1997

CHIMAIRA / ROADRUNNER RECORDS / 2001

DÅÅTH / ROADRUNNER RECORDS / 2004

DEVIL DRIVER / ROADRUNNER RECORDS / 2003

ADEMA / *PLANETS* / EARACHE RECORDS / 2005

THE HAUNTED / EARACHE RECORDS / 1998

ICED EARTH / CENTURY MEDIA RECORDS / JON SCHAFFER / 1991

NAPALM DEATH / EARACHE RECORDS / 1987

DEATH / COMBAT RECORDS / CHUCK SCHULDINER / 1985

CENTINEX / CANDLELIGHT RECORDS / KETOLA / 2001

EMPEROR / CANDLELIGHT RECORDS / 1993

MORDA / *AZERION* / EYE SPY RECORDS / 2005

MORTIIS / *SOME KIND OF HEROIN* / EARACHE RECORDS / 2007

NORA / *DREAMERS & DEADMEN* / TRUSTKILL RECORDS / JACOB BANNON / 2003

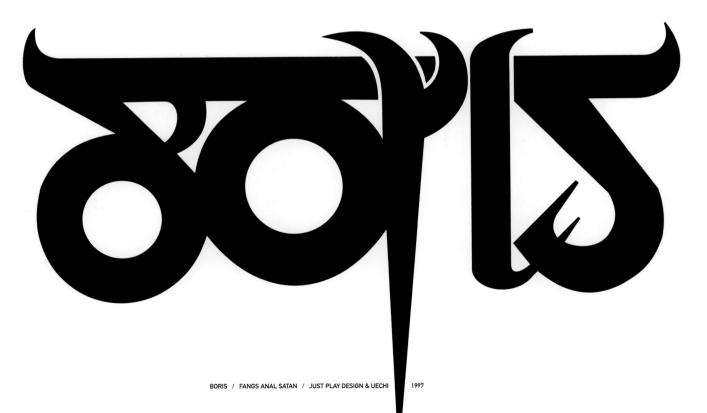

BORIS / FANGS ANAL SATAN / JUST PLAY DESIGN & UECHI / 1997

LAMB OF GOD / METAL BLADE RECORDS / 2000

SUNN O))) / SOUTHERN LORD RECORDS / STEPHEN O'MALLEY / 2003

KREATOR / NOISE RECORDS / 1985

EXODUS / COMBAT RECORDS / 1982

DESTRUCTION / STEAMHAMMER RECORDS / 1985

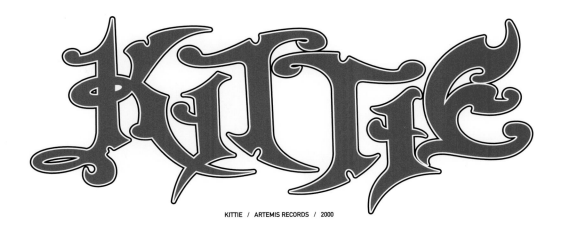

KITTIE / ARTEMIS RECORDS / 2000

KATATONIA / *DANCE OF DECEMBER SOULS* / NO FASHION RECORDS / 1993

KATATONIA / *DISCOURAGED ONES* / AVANTGARDE MUSIC / 1998

ARMORED SAINT / METAL BLADE RECORDS / 1983

KING DIAMOND  /  ROADRUNNER RECORDS  /  1986

SLAYER / METAL BLADE RECORDS / STEVE CRAIG / 1983

SLAYER / *DIVINE INTERVENTION* / AMERICAN RECORDINGS / 1991

SLAYER / *GOD HATES US ALL* / AMERICAN RECORDINGS / 2001

SLAYER / *SHOW NO MERCY* / METAL BLADE RECORDS / STEVE CRAIG / 1983

DEATHWITCH / EWIGKEIT / EXMORTEM / DECAPITATED / CALLISTO / CATHEDRAL / CARCASS / EXTREME NOISE TERROR / ENTOMBED / HATE ETERNAL / USURPER / THE CHASM / EARACHE RECORDS

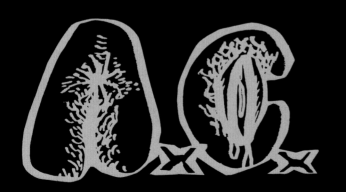

MUNICIPAL WASTE / INSISION / LOST SOUL / ANATA / ANAL CUNT / NOX / EARACHE RECORDS

DEATHBED ATHEIST / INVISIBLE CREATURE / 2005

BECOMING THE ARCHETYPE / *THE PHYSICS OF FIRE* / SOLID STATE RECORDS / INVISIBLE CREATURE / 2007

IT DIES TODAY / *SIRENS* / TRUSTKILL RECORDS / SONS OF NERO / 2006

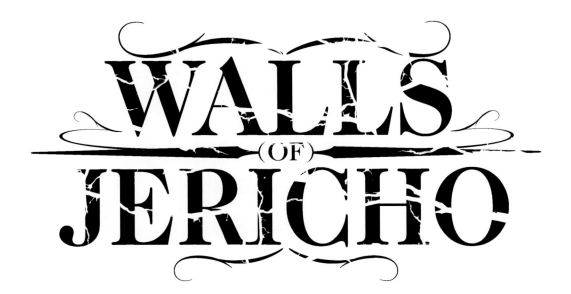

WALLS OF JERICHO / *WITH DEVILS AMONGST US ALL* / TRUSTKILL RECORDS / ADAM WENTWORTH / 2006

OPETH / CANDLELIGHT RECORDS / TIMO KETOLA / 1996

MESHUGGAH / *NOTHING* / NUCLEAR BLAST RECORDS / 2002

MASTODON / *BLOOD MOUNTAIN* / REPRISE RECORDS / PAUL A. ROMANO / 2006

SEVENDUST / *ANIMOSITY* / TVT RECORDS / DANIEL TREMONTI / 2001

MUDVAYNE / *LOST AND FOUND* / EPIC RECORDS / AIMÉE MACAULLEY / 2005

BEDLIGHT FOR BLUE EYES / TRUSTKILL RECORDS / TIMOTHY LEO / 2005

KILLING THE DREAM / RIVALRY RECORDS / 2006

MAYLENE & THE SONS OF DISASTER / MONO VS STEREO / INVISIBLE CREATURE / 2005

TRIVIUM / ROADRUNNER RECORDS / PAUL A. ROMANO / 2005

SANCTUARY / EPIC RECORDS / ED REPKA / 1987

DRY KILL LOGIC / ROADRUNNER RECORDS / 2001

KILLSWITCH ENGAGE  /  ROADRUNNER RECORDS  /  2005

NECROPHAGIST / RELAPSE RECORDS / 2004

NECROPHOBIC / BLACK MARK PRODUCTION / JOHAN HANSSON / 1993

# TRUE PUNK ICON

How many punks have scrawled Winston Smith's logo for the Dead Kennedys on their school notebooks, carved it into their desks, or Sharpied it onto bathroom stalls? At its simplest, you only have to be able to draw four lines, and there you have it: Instant punk logo.

San Francisco–based artist/anarchist Smith met Dead Kennedys lead singer Jello Biafra in 1979 after Biafra had seen Smith's painting "Cross of Money" (later used for the cover art of the band's *In God We Trust, Inc.*). Smith formed a lasting relationship with the band, designing the iconic logo and six of the DKs' album covers, along with numerous covers, flyers, and logos for Biafra's record label Alternative Tentacles. Smith also contributed the cover art for Green Day's *Insomniac* and the Burning Brides' *Leave No Ashes*, in addition to amassing a significant body of collage works.

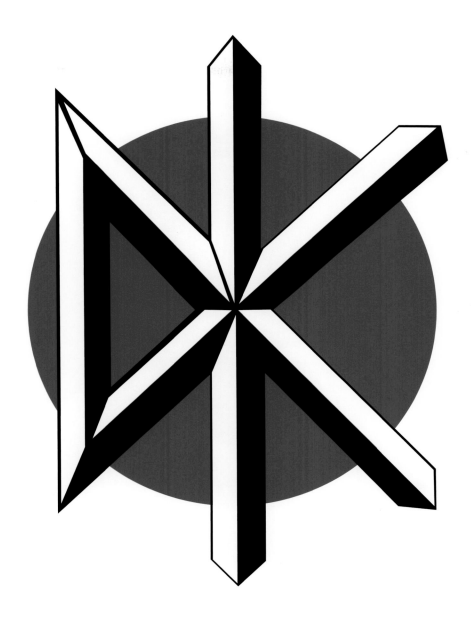

DEAD KENNEDYS / ALTERNATIVE TENTACLES RECORDS / WINSTON SMITH / 1981

CORROSION OF CONFORMITY / DEATH RECORDS / 1989

ANTI-NOWHERE LEAGUE / *OUT OF CONTROL* / RECEIVER RECORDS / 1993

# RAMONES

RAMONES / SIRE RECORDS / ARTURO VEGA / 1977

NIRVANA / SUB POP RECORDS / LISA ORTH & GRANT ALDEN / 1989

# Turbonegro

TURBONEGRO / *APOCALYPSE DUDES* / MAN'S RUIN RECORDS / 1999

# TURBONEGRO

TURBONEGRO / *SCANDINAVIAN LEATHER* / BURNING HEART RECORDS / JAGGED DESIGN / 2003

# THE DISTILLERS

THE DISTILLERS / HELLCAT RECORDS / 2002

RIVERBOAT GAMBLERS / VOLCOM ENTERTAINMENT / 2006

LEFT ALONE / *LONELY STARTS & BROKEN HEARTS* / HELLCAT RECORDS / 2005

THE AQUABATS / GOLDENVOICE RECORDINGS / 1997

THE CREPIDS / HELLSIDE RECORDS / CREPID J. LEVY / 1991

THE CREPIDS / HELLSIDE RECORDS / CREPID J. LEVY / 1992

DISSONANCE / HELLSIDE RECORDS / CREPID J. LEVY / 1990

ADOLE-
SCENTS

THE ADOLESCENTS / FRONTIER RECORDS / DIANE ZINCAVAGE / 1981

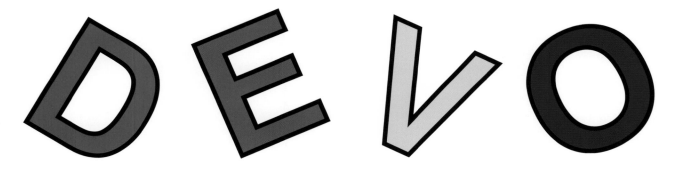

BULLET LAVOLTA / *THE GIFT* / TAANG! RECORDS / 1989

DEVO / WARNER BROS. RECORDS / ERIK MUNSÖN / 1978

ME FIRST AND THE GIMME GIMMES / FAT WRECK CHORDS / 1997

# FOUR BARS

Greg Ginn founded the seminal hardcore punk band Black Flag in 1977, and enlisted his brother Raymond Pettibon—then a former high school teacher, budding artist, and one-time bandmate of Greg in Black Flag's precursor, Panic—to design their logo. Neither Ginn nor Pettibon knew at the time that both the music and the logo would irrevocably change the punk scene, but they acted as if it could (as Pettibon pointed out, the name had reference to an anarchist symbol, an insect repellent, and Black Sabbath all rolled into one). On stage, Black Flag pushed the boundaries of intensity, angst, and aggression, while on the streets Pettibon's "Four Bars" logo spread like a virus, tattooed onto shoulders and calves and graffitied onto walls and signs throughout Los Angeles. The bold yet simple geometric symbol, which represented a waving black flag divided into vertical bars, also represented all things punk in SoCal. When front man Keith Morris left Black Flag (and went on to form the Circle Jerks), the vacuum left by his departure was finally filled by the addition in 1981 of Henry Rollins, a rabid twenty-year-old fan whose primal ferocity and vein-bulging, muscle-baring tirades would come to define the band's hardcore image.

As for Pettibon, after working on Black Flag's early flyers and album covers and working with other bands such as the Minutemen and Sonic Youth (notably for their album *Goo*) as well as publishing books, his interests and exposure eventually expanded outside the punk world and into the international art scene. He is known for monochromatic works, mostly in ink, and has also worked in video art and installations, with his art exhibited at L.A.'s Museum of Contemporary Art, the Whitney Museum of American Art, and the Venice Biennale.

BLACK FLAG / SST RECORDS / RAYMOND PETTIBON / 1978

SHATTERED FAITH  /  POSH BOY RECORDS  /  1981

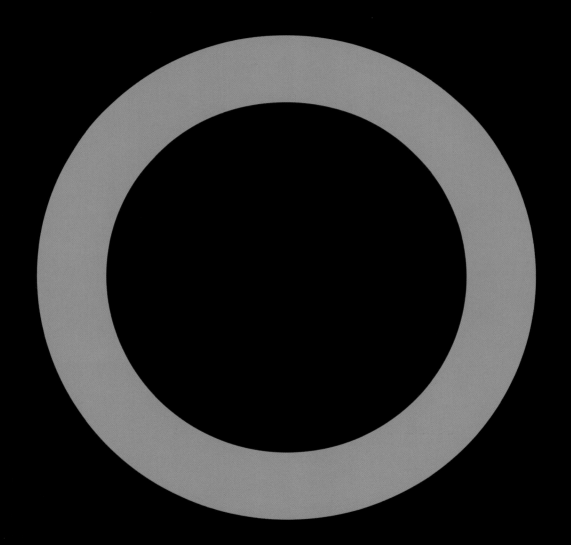

THE GERMS / SLASH RECORDS / DON BOLLES & DARBY CRASH / 1978

DAG NASTY / DISCHORD RECORDS / CYNTHIA CONNOLLY / 1987

NEW YORK DOLLS / MERCURY RECORDS / 1973

THE MISFITS / PLAN B RECORDS / GLENN DANZIG / 1981

# DESCENDENTS

THE EXPLOITED / *LET'S START A WAR* / COMBAT RECORDS / PUSHEAD / 1983

# 7 SECONDS

7 SECONDS / *SOULFORCE REVOLUTION* / RESTLESS RECORDS / KEVIN SECONDS / 1993

SENSES FAIL / VAGRANT RECORDS / 2006

7 SECONDS / KEVIN SECONDS / 1980

R.K.L / MYSTIC RECORDS / DAN SITES / 1984

GG ALLIN / *YOU GIVE LOVE A BAD NAME* / AWARE ONE RECORDS / 1987

SUICIDAL TENDENCIES / FRONTIER RECORDS / GLEN E. FRIEDMAN / 1982

DIE HUNNS / *YOU ROT ME* / VOLCOM ENTERTAINMENT / 2006

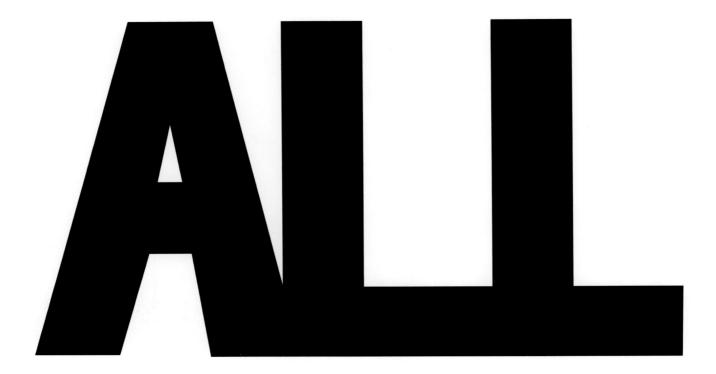

ALL / CRUZ RECORDS / 1988

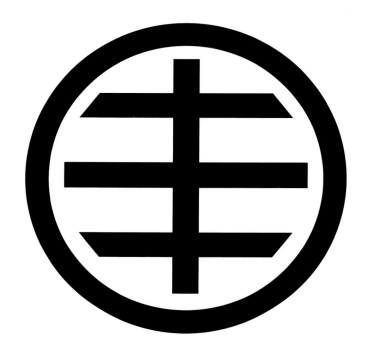

HÜSKER DÜ / SST RECORDS / 1981

THE BUZZCOCKS / UNITED ARTISTS RECORDS / MALCOLM GARRETT / 1978

# RISE AGAINST

RISE AGAINST / *THIS IS NOISE* / GEFFEN RECORDS / 2007

# BAD RELIGION

BAD RELIGION / EPITAPH RECORDS / 1981

D.O.A. / *SOMETHING BETTER CHANGE* / CAN. FRIENDS RECORDS / 1980

D.R.I. / METAL BLADE RECORDS / 1985

THE CLASH / *GIVE 'EM ENOUGH ROPE* / EPIC RECORDS / GENE GREIF / 1978

THE CLASH / CBS RECORDS / 1977

**THE EXPLOITED**

THE EXPLOITED / *BEAT THE BASTARDS* / ROUGH JUSTICE RECORDS / 1996

THE CRAMPS / ILLEGAL RECORDS / LUX INTERIOR & IVY RORSCHACH / 1979

THE CRAMPS / LOGO FOR TOUR POSTER / ART CHANTRY / 1997

PUBLIC IMAGE LTD / VIRGIN RECORDS / DENNIS MORRIS & JOHN LYDON / 1979

SEX PISTOLS / VIRGIN RECORDS / HELEN OF TROY & JAMIE REID / 1977

With its cut-and-paste collage-style lettering of different sizes and fonts, the Sex Pistols' logo had the look of a ransom note—antiauthoritarian, dangerous, anarchic, bordering on psychotic. Just like the band. Jamie Reed's logo debuted in July 1977 for the single "God Save the Queen" and was reportedly based on a blackmail-style design originally executed by Malcolm McLaren's dwarf friend Helen of Troy for the band's gig flyers.

FEAR / SLASH RECORDS / 1981

LARS FREDERIKSEN AND THE BASTARDS  /  HELLCAT RECORDS  /  2001

FENIX TX  /  MCA RECORDS  /  1999

ROGER MIRET AND THE DISASTERS  /  HELLCAT RECORDS  /  2002

NEKROMANTIX  /  *HELLBOUND*  /  TOMBSTONE RECORDS  /  1989

TIME AGAIN / HELLCAT RECORDS / 2006

SURF PUNKS / *LOCALS ONLY* / RESTLESS RECORDS / MARK MILLER / 1982

RANCID / EPITAPH RECORDS / MACKIE / 1993

LAGWAGON / FAT WRECK CHORDS / 1994

THE OFFSPRING / *SPLINTER* / COLUMBIA RECORDS / STORM THORGERSON & PETER CURZON / 2003

GUTTERMOUTH / *SHAVE THE PLANET* / VOLCOM ENTERTAINMENT / RYAN IMMEGART / 2006

THE DAMNED / *GRAVE DISORDER* / NITRO RECORDS / 2001

BUTTHOLE SURFERS / TOUCH & GO RECORDS / GIBBY HAYNES / 1988

THE FARTZ / ALTERNATIVE TENTACLES / 1981

CIRCLE JERKS / FRONTIER RECORDS / DOUG DRUG / 1980

THE DICKS / *THE DICKS HATE THE POLICE* / RADICAL RECORDS / CARLOS LOWRY / 1980

MINOR THREAT / DISCHORD RECORDS / JEFF NELSON / 1981

BAD BRAINS / *ROCK FOR LIGHT* / PVC RECORDS / 1983

BAD BRAINS / ROIR RECORDS / DAVID LEE PARSONS / 1982

BAD BRAINS / *I AGAINST I* / SST RECORDS / PAUL BACON STUDIO / 1986

MXPX / A&M RECORDS / INVISIBLE CREATURE / 2003

JFA / PLACEBO RECORDS / 1983

THE STOOGES / ELEKTRA RECORDS / WILLIAM S. HARVEY / 1969

# KRAUT

KRAUT / *AN ADJUSTMENT TO SOCIETY* / CABBAGE RECORDS / 1982

# NAKED RAYGUN

NAKED RAYGUN / HOMESTEAD RECORDS / 1983

# DICKS

THE DICKS / *KILL FROM THE HEART* / SST RECORDS / CARLOS LOWRY / 1983

TOKEN ENTRY / *WEIGHT OF THE WORLD* / EMERGO RECORDS / 1990

GORILLA BISCUITS / REVELATION RECORDS / ALEX BROWN / 1988

PENNYWISE / EPITAPH RECORDS / FRED HIDALGO / 1992

CRASS / SMALL WONDER RECORDS / DAVE KING / 1978

BLINK-182 / MCA RECORDS / TIM STEDMAN / 1999

BLINK-182 / GEFFEN RECORDS / 2003

BLINK-182 / GEFFEN RECORDS / TRAVIS BARKER / 2003

NOFX / *SO LONG AND THANKS FOR ALL THE SHOES* / EPITAPH RECORDS / 1997

NOFX / *PUMP UP THE VALUUM* / EPITAPH RECORDS / 2000

NOFX / *WOLVES IN WOLVES' CLOTHING* / FAT WRECK CHORDS / 2006

GREEN DAY  /  *NIMROD*  /  REPRISE RECORDS  /  CHRIS BILHEIMER  /  1997

GREEN DAY  /  *KERPLUNK!*  /  LOOKOUT RECORDS  /  CHRIS APPELCORE  /  1992

GREEN DAY  /  *WARNING*  /  REPRISE RECORDS  /  CHRIS BILHEIMER  /  2000

THE RICH / *SIMPLE ECONOMICS* / FERALMEDIA / SOPPCOLLECTIVE / 2005

THE BREEDERS / LOGO FOR POSTER / ART CHANTRY / 2003

THE FALLS / *LONG TIME COMING* / SOPPCOLLECTIVE / 2007

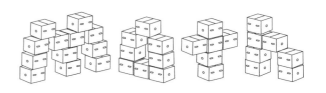

UNREST / *PERFECT TEETH* / 4AD / CHRIS BIGG / 1993

KULA SHAKER / *K* / COLUMBIA RECORDS / STYLOROUGE / 1996

MOTH / VIRGIN RECORDS / KARLSSONWILKER INC. / 2002

NEUTRAL MILK HOTEL / MERGE RECORDS / CHRIS BILHEIMER / 1998

HURON / COMO PARK MUSIC / STYLOROUGE / 2005

SUM 41 / *DOES THIS LOOK INFECTED?* / ISLAND RECORDS / MORNING BREATH INC. / 2002

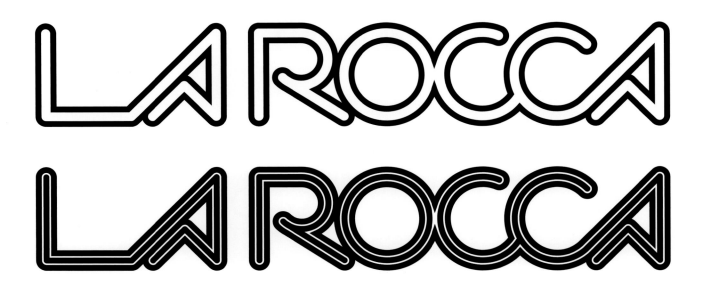

LA ROCCA / *SING SONG SUNG* / DANGERBIRD RECORDS / SMOG DESIGN / RYAN COREY / 2006

THE VINES / CAPITOL RECORDS / KARLSSONWILKER INC. / 2002

AUF DER MAUR / CAPITOL RECORDS / KARLSSONWILKER INC. / 2003

DANKO JONES  /  BAD TASTE RECORDS  /  HENRIK WALSE  /  2003

OF MONTREAL  /  KINDERCORE RECORDS  /  CHRIS BILHEIMER  /  1998

THE VON BONDIES / SIRE RECORDS / INVISIBLE CREATURE / 2003

ALL LOGOS: R.E.M. / WARNER BROS. RECORDS / CHRIS BILHEIMER / 1993–2007

# INTERVIEW WITH CHRIS BILHEIMER

Athens, Georgia–based designer Chris Bilheimer was just graduating college in the early '90s when his friendship with Michael Stipe evolved into a job as R.E.M.'s full-time art director. Over the years, this lasting relationship has led to numberous logo variations, tens of millions of CDs sold, and two Grammy nominations in the Best Album Packaging category.

In addition to his work with R.E.M., Chris also works on a free-lance basis for top bands like Green Day, Smashing Pumpkins, Foo Fighters, and Weezer, and has designed corporate logos for DreamWorks, Outpost Records, and SingleCell Films. Chris is also keen with a camera, and his band photography has been featured in magazines such as *Rolling Stone* and *Raygun*.

• What's your background? Did you go to design school?

I never went to design school. I was getting a BFA in Drawing/Painting and started to teach myself how to use the Mac so I could make flyers for a friend's band. The art school at UGA (in Athens) has a Mac lab that was open to non-design students after hours. Around 1992, I just started going in there and stumbling through Photoshop and Freehand and teaching myself.

• How did the relationship with R.E.M. start?

I met Michael Stipe in 1988 through a mutual friend. I was supposed to meet him after the last show of the *Green* tour, but we got lost in the bowels of the Macon Coliseum and didn't meet him until days later. I wasn't hired as official band "art director" until the end of 1993. I had driven across the country with Michael that year, and he wanted to do a T-shirt based on a road sign that we had seen. I designed the shirt and it went really smoothly. I then was hired to assist Michael in designing everything and coordinating with Tom Recchion at Warner Bros., who had been doing their design for a couple of years.

• Do you collaborate with Michael Stipe on everything? What about the other guys in the band, do they get a say in the final results?

We collaborate on everything. Over the years I have had a bigger hand in what they put out, but it is always a collaboration. Sometimes it is 90 percent his ideas, sometimes 90 percent mine. It is different every time, which keeps it interesting. The rest of the band pretty much leaves it up to us, as long as they get to approve all the photographs of them.

• Tell me about re-designing the identity of the same band over the years. Each album has a different logo type treatment on it. Do you work on the logo design first, and then shape the rest of the album design around it, or do you and the band have a general feel for the "look" of the album, and then steer the logo design in that direction?

Well, it is different every time. Sometimes we are inspired by the typography, and sometimes the typography is really secondary. It really just depends on where the original inspiration came from. For *New Adventures In Hi-Fi*, the band settled on a black-and-white photograph to fit the mood of the record, so there was really no logo, just really minimal plain type.

• How often do you run into creative problems with the powers that be?

I feel lucky that I get to do this for a living, so I usually don't get too confrontational about projects. I see my job as to help the artist express themselves, so I leave myself out of it. It seems kind of egotistical to tell a band how they should present themselves. I mean, I get pissed off every now and then, but who doesn't?

• Some people might say "R.E.M. is three letters, how hard could it be to type it in a different font and call it a logo?"

Well, it keeps me from misspelling it. The record *Hi-Fi* was just a font, but that was the point. Overall, I try really hard to take a logo somewhere beyond just being a font, whether it means altering the type, or spray-painting it, or Xeroxing it 500 times. I feel kinda lame if I just use a font.

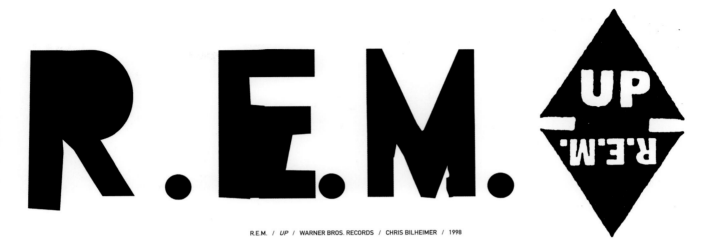

R.E.M. / *UP* / WARNER BROS. RECORDS / CHRIS BILHEIMER / 1998

• Which one of the R.E.M. logos is your personal favorite?

Maybe the one from *UP*, or the typeface for *In Time*, which I made myself, very poorly. It would kern for shit.

• You've also done a lot of work and multiple logos for Green Day. How did that relationship come about?

I met Billie Joe at an R.E.M. show in San Francisco. We became friends for a few years, but I didn't work with them, mainly because they try to not work with friends because it can often put a strain on everything. But during the making of *Nimrod* (released in 1997), they went through three art directors and were desperate. I got called at the last minute, and everything worked out really well. I have been doing all their work since then.

• Do you have any idea how many albums have been sold with your logos on them? How does it feel knowing that your work is sitting on millions and millions of people's shelves at home?

I have no idea, really. Probably around 25 to 30 million copies? It is a little strange, because I still live in a small town in Georgia, and I am pretty cut off from the industry. I design things and e-mail them off, and maybe see them here or there. It's not like I drive by huge billboards of my work every day. I did see some Green Day shirts I designed in Target the other day, and that was weird.

• Between R.E.M. and Green Day, does that leave you time to work with other bands?

Yeah. I love what I do, so I keep really busy. I do a lot of design for free for local bands, as well as indie and major label stuff (Weezer, All-American Rejects, Yellowcard, Buckcherry). I always have something going on. I get bored really easily if I don't.

• Do you design mostly for music?

I have been doing a lot of comedy stuff. I did a book and tour merchandise for [the HBO program] *Mr. Show*. I have also designed comedy albums for Sarah Silverman, Greg Behrendt, Patton Oswalt and the Comedians of Comedy. That has been really fun to get to add some humor to my work. For Sarah Silverman's album, I got to draw her riding a unicorn on a rainbow while farting stars! Probably my career highlight.

• Lastly, what are your favorite band logos?

Well, the Rolling Stones' logo has probably made my job harder than any other logo. Bands will always say "We want something iconic, like the lips and tongue. You know, it doesn't even have to say their name but you know who it is." I want to shoot myself in the face every time I hear that. Otherwise, I don't really have any favorite logos that come to mind.

THE SISTERS OF MERCY  /  MERCIFUL RELEASE  /  1980

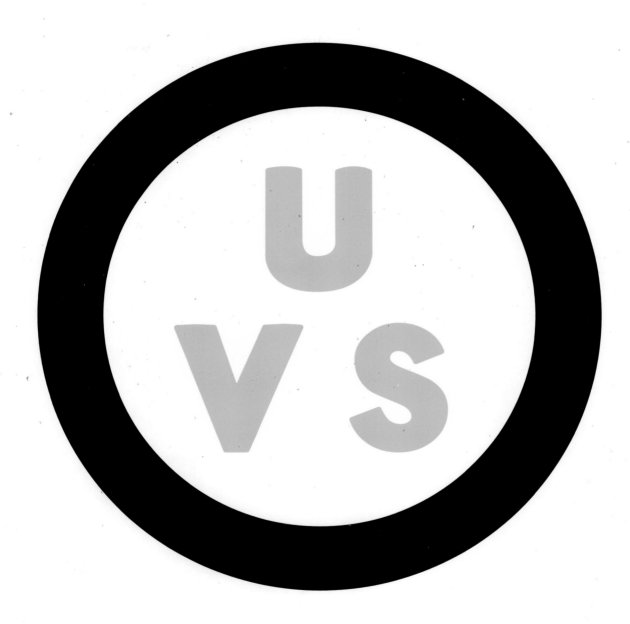

ULTRA VIVID SCENE  /  4AD RECORDS  /  VAUGHAN OLIVER  /  1988

SNOW PATROL

SNOW PATROL / *FINAL STRAW* / POLYDOR UK / 2003

ARCADE FIRE / MERGE RECORDS / 2003

SCISSOR SISTERS

SCISSOR SISTERS / POLYDOR RECORDS / 2004

FORTY FOOT ECHO

FORTY FOOT ECHO / HOLLYWOOD RECORDS / T42DESIGN / 2003

PETER WALKER / *YOUNG GRAVITY* / DANGERBIRD RECORDS / SMOG DESIGN / SARA CUMINGS / 2006

GENERAL PUBLIC / I.R.S. RECORDS / 1984

PEPPER / VOLCOM ENTERTAINMENT / BEN BROUGH / 2000

SUBLIME / *SECOND HAND SMOKE* / GASOLINE ALLEY RECORDS / OPIE GIBRAN ORTIZ / 1997

THE SPECIALS / 2 TONE RECORDS / 1979

FISHBONE / COLUMBIA RECORDS / TONY LANE & NANCY DONALD / 1985

THE ENGLISH BEAT / *SPECIAL BEAT SERVICE* / I.R.S. RECORDS / 1990

THE UNTOUCHABLES / *LIVE AND LET DANCE* / TWIST RECORDS / ROBERT FUSFIELD & RICK NEWSOME / 1984

THE ENGLISH BEAT / *I JUST CAN'T STOP IT* / I.R.S. RECORDS / 1980

THE SELECTER / *TOO MUCH PRESSURE* / 2 TONE RECORDS / 1980

RADIOHEAD / *THE BENDS* / CAPITOL RECORDS / 1995

**molotov**

MOLOTOV / *DANCE AND DENSE DENSO* / UNIVERSAL MUSIC LATINO / 2003

SIGUE SIGUE SPUTNIK / SPUTNIKWORLD RECORDS / 2002

SECONDSTOMARS

30 SECONDS TO MARS / VIRGIN RECORDS / 2006

THE B-52'S / WARNER BROS. RECORDS / 1979

ELASTICA / GEFFEN RECORDS / 1995

SUGARPLUM FAIRY / COLUMBIA RECORDS / HENRIK WALSE / 2005

MASSIVE ATTACK / *BLUE LINES* / VIRGIN RECORDS / 3D-DEL NAJA & MICHAEL NASH / 1991

SIMPLE MINDS / *LIVE IN THE CITY OF LIGHT* / VIRGIN RECORDS / MICK HAGGERTY / 1987

MORRISSEY / ATTACK RECORDS / STYLOROUGE / 2006

MORRISSEY / *RINGLEADER OF THE TORMENTORS* / ATTACK RECORDS / STYLOROUGE / 2006

SPACEMEN 3 / GLASS RECORDS / 1986

THE JESUS AND MARY CHAIN / BLANCO Y NEGRO / STYLOROUGE / 1994

SIMPLE MINDS / *REAL LIFE* / A&M RECORDS / STYLOROUGE / 1991

LEVEL 42 / *RUNNING IN THE FAMILY* / POLYGRAM RECORDS / 1987

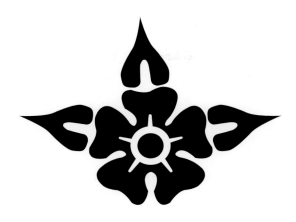

THE ORDINARY BOYS / B UNIQUE RECORDS / STYLOROUGE / 2005

311 / CAPRICORN RECORDS / 1994

SKINNY PUPPY / SYNTHETIC SYMPHONY / STEVEN R. GILMORE / 2004

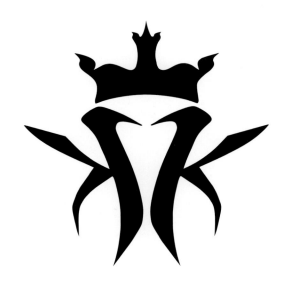

KOTTONMOUTH KINGS / COLUMBIA RECORDS / 1998

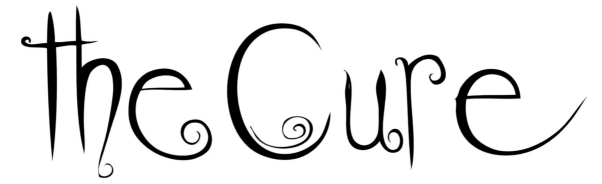

THE CURE / *KISS ME, KISS ME, KISS ME* / ELECTRA RECORDS / VELLA DESIGN / 1987

LUCKY JIM / SKINT RECORDS / RED DESIGN UK LTD. / 2006

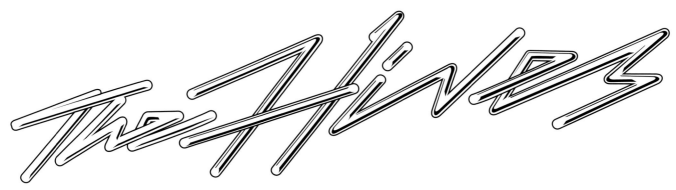

THE HIVES / LOGO FOR TOUR MATERIALS / INTERSCOPE RECORDS / HENRIK WALSE / 2005

FOREVER LIKE RED / THE ECHO LABEL LIMITED / RED DESIGN UK LTD. / 2007

# Spiritualized®

SPIRITUALIZED / *LADIES AND GENTLEMEN WE ARE FLOATING IN SPACE* / ARISTA RECORDS / 1997

GENE LOVES JEZEBEL / BEGGARS UK / 1983

WEEN / *GOD WEEN SATAN: THE ONENESS* / TWIN TONE RECORDS / 1990

HOLE / "DICKNAIL" B/W "BURNBLACK" (SINGLE) / SUB POP RECORDS / ART CHANTRY, BRUCE PAVITT & COURTNEY LOVE / 1991

HOLE / *LIVE THROUGH THIS* / GEFFEN RECORDS / 1994

BELLY / 4AD RECORDS / CHRIS BIGG / 1993

LUSH / 4AD RECORDS / VAUGHAN OLIVER & CHRIS BIGG / 1994

ENGERICA

THERE ARE NO HAPPY ENDINGS

ENGERICA / *THERE ARE NO HAPPY ENDINGS* / SANCTUARY RECORDS / STYLOROUGE / 2006

ALPEN / *OVERDUB* / FERAL MEDIA / SOPP COLLECTIVE / 2005

THE MODERN LOVERS / BESERKLEY RECORDS / 1976

THE STROKES  /  RCA RECORDS  /  2001

OZOMATLI / ALMO SOUNDS / LUIS RAMIREZ / 1998

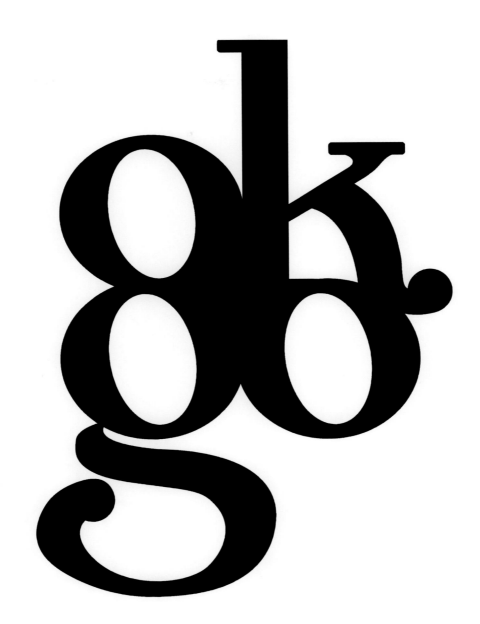

OK GO / *OH NO* / CAPITOL RECORDS / 2005

THE THE  /  EPIC RECORDS / FIONA SKINNER  /  1983

DEPECHE MODE  /  *EXCITER*  /  MUTE RECORDS  /  FORM®  /  2001

DAVE GAHAN  /  *PAPER MONSTERS*  /  MUTE RECORDS  /  FOURFIVEONECREATIVE  /  2003

BLONDIE / *PARALLEL LINES* / CHRYSALIS RECORDS / JERRY RODRIGUEZ / 1978

DEPECHE MODE / *VIOLATOR* / MUTE RECORDS / AREA / 1990

GORILLAZ / VIRGIN RECORDS / JAMIE HEWLETT / 2001

SIGUR RÓS / *( )* / FATCAT RECORDS / 2001

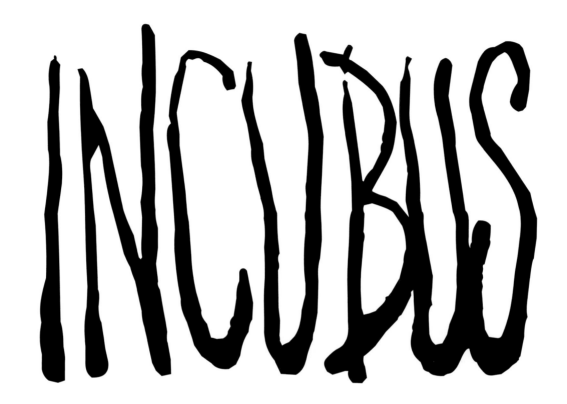

INCUBUS / *A CROW LEFT OF THE MURDER* / EPIC RECORDS / BRANDY FLOWER / 2004

INCUBUS / *LIGHT GRENADES* / EPIC RECORDS / 2006

REEL BIG FISH  /  *OUR LIVE ALBUM IS BETTER THAN YOUR LIVE ALBUM*  /  ROCK RIDGE MUSIC  /  2006

BIRDS OF AVALON  /  *BAZAAR BAZAAR*  /  VOLCOM ENTERTAINMENT  /  2007

MOGWAI / *ROCK ACTION* / MATADOR RECORDS / VELLA DESIGN / 2001

MOTION CITY SOUNDTRACK / EPITAPH RECORDS / NICK PRITCHARD / 2005

ThePresidents
ofTheUnitedSt
atesofAmerica

THE PRESIDENTS OF THE UNITED STATES OF AMERICA / COLUMBIA RECORDS / ART CHANTRY / 1995

YELLOWCARD / *LIGHTS AND SOUNDS* / CAPITOL RECORDS / CHRIS BILHEIMER / 2006

JESUS JONES / FOOD RECORDS / STYLOROUGE / 1989

TIGER ARMY / HELLCAT RECORDS / 2004

# bauhaus

BAUHAUS / BEGGARS BANQUET RECORDS / 1982

PIXIES / 4AD RECORDS / VAUGHAN OLIVER / 1991

RED HOT CHILI PEPPERS / EMI RECORDS / 1988

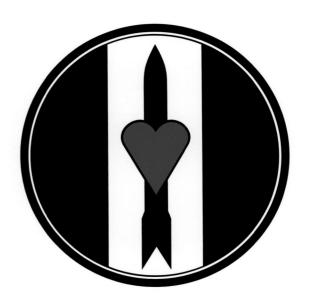

LOVE AND ROCKETS / BEGGARS BANQUET RECORDS / 1985

HARVEY DANGER / LOGO FOR TOUR T-SHIRT / ART CHANTRY / 1998

URGE OVERKILL / TOUCH AND GO RECORDS / 1990

IVY / LEAVES T-SHIRT LOGO / NETTWERK RECORDS / JASON MUNN / 2004

ANGELS & AIRWAVES / GEFFEN RECORDS / TOM DELONGE / 2005

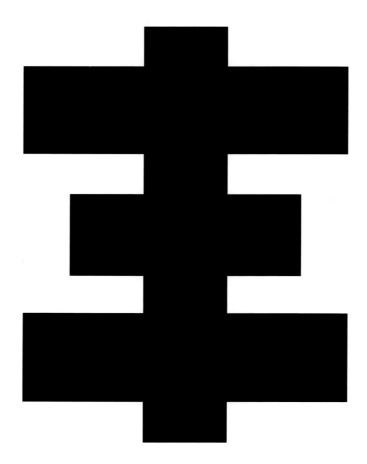

# PSYCHIC TV

PSYCHIC TV / TEMPLE RECORDS / GENESIS P-ORRIDGE / 1982

# RADIOHEAD

RADIOHEAD / *KID A* / PARLOPHONE RECORDS / 2000

# MUSE

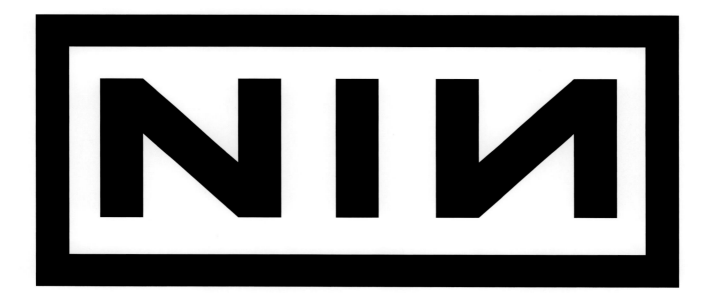

NINE INCH NAILS / TVT RECORDS / GARY TALPAS & TRENT REZNOR / 1989

Nine Inch Nails mastermind Trent Reznor and designer Gary Talpas collaborated on the unforgettably simple, strikingly bold NIN palindrome logo in 1988. Reznor sought a compact insignia for his leather jacket sleeve, and he was inspired by the inverted letter A used by Tibor Kalman for the typography of the Talking Heads' 1980 *Remain in Light* album cover (see page 305). Talpas and Reznor also collaborated on much of NIN's packaging and design.

# SCATTER**THE**ASHES

SCATTER THE ASHES / EPITAPH RECORDS / NICK PRITCHARD / 2004

# THE MUSIC

THE MUSIC / HUT RECORDINGS / LINDA BARITSKI / 2001

MONO / *FORMICA BLUES* / ECHO RECORDS / BLUESOURCE / 1997

# THE SMITHS

THE SMITHS / *MEAT IS MURDER* / ROUGH TRADE RECORDS / MORRISSEY & CARYN GOUGH / 1985

# THE WEAKERTHANS

THE WEAKERTHANS / *RECONSTRUCTION SITE* / EPITAPH RECORDS / MIKE CAROLL / 2003

# TALKINGHEADS

TALKING HEADS / *REMAIN IN LIGHT* / SIRE RECORDS / TIBOR KALMAN / 1980

# THE CARDIGANS

THE CARDIGANS / *LAST BAND ON THE MOON* / STOCKHOLM RECORDS / MARTIN RENCK / 1996

# SLEATER-KINNEY

SLEATER-KINNEY / *THE WOODS* / SUB POP RECORDS / JEFF KLEINSMITH / 2004

THE ALL-AMERICAN REJECTS / INTERSCOPE RECORDS / MADEBYGREGG / 2003

THE ALL-AMERICAN REJECTS / INTERSCOPE RECORDS / INVISIBLE CREATURE / 2004

THE ALL-AMERICAN REJECTS / INTERSCOPE RECORDS / INVISIBLE CREATURE / 2006

THE ALL-AMERICAN REJECTS / *MOVE ALONG* / INTERSCOPE RECORDS / CHRIS BILHEIMER / 2005

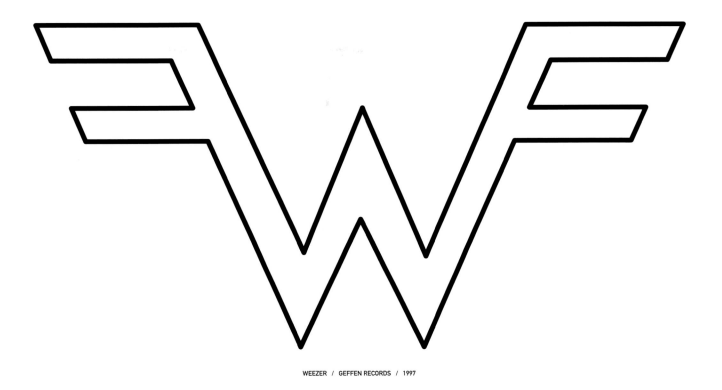

WEEZER / GEFFEN RECORDS / 1997

WEEZER / GEFFEN RECORDS / FRANCESCA RESTREPO / 1994

**blur**

BLUR / EMI RECORDS / STYLOROUGE / 1991

*BLUR*

BLUR / *LIVE AT THE BUDOKAN* / EMI RECORDS / 1996

Mystery Jets

MYSTERY JETS / "ALAS AGNES" (SINGLE) / 679 RECORDINGS / STYLOROUGE / 2005

# MYSTERY JETS

MYSTERY JETS / "THE BOY WHO RAN AWAY" (SINGLE) / 679 RECORDINGS / STYLOROUGE / 2006

JYROJETS / SONGPHONIC RECORDS / STYLOROUGE / 2006

# JET

JET / *GET BORN* / ELEKTRA RECORDS / GREG GIGENDAD BURKE / 2003

# THE POSTAL SERVICE

THE POSTAL SERVICE / *GIVE UP* / SUB POP RECORDS / JEFF KLEINSMITH / 2003

# TALKING HEADS: 77

TALKING HEADS / *TALKING HEADS: 77* / SIRE RECORDS / DAVID BYRNE / 1977

# smashing pumpkins

THE SMASHING PUMPKINS / *SIAMESE DREAM* / VIRGIN RECORDS / STEVE GERDES / 1993

# The Smashing Pumpkins

THE SMASHING PUMPKINS / *MELLON COLLIE AND THE INFINITE SADNESS* / VIRGIN RECORDS / FRANK OLINSKY / 1995

VAUX / *BEYOND VIRTUE, BEYOND VICE* / OUTLOOK MUSIC / QUENTIN SMITH / 2006

SUGARCUBES / *STICK AROUND FOR JOY* / ONE LITTLE INDIAN RECORDS / ME COMPANY / 1992

BJÖRK / *DEBUT* / ONE LITTLE INDIAN RECORDS / ME COMPANY / 1993

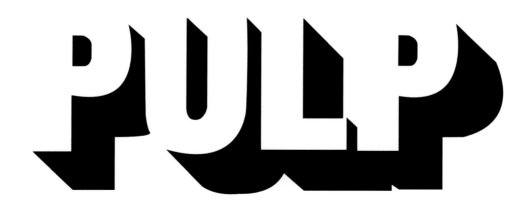

PULP / *THIS IS HARDCORE* / ISLAND RECORDS / PETER SAVILLE / 1998

MUDHONEY / *PIECE OF CAKE* / REPRISE RECORDS / ART CHANTRY / 1992

MUDHONEY / *UNDER A BILLION SUNS* / SUB POP RECORDS / JEFF KLEINSMITH / 2006

MR. BUNGLE / WARNER BROS. RECORDS / 1991

the goo goo dolls let love in

GOO GOO DOLLS / *LET LOVE IN* / WARNER BROS. RECORDS / MORNING BREATH INC. / 2006

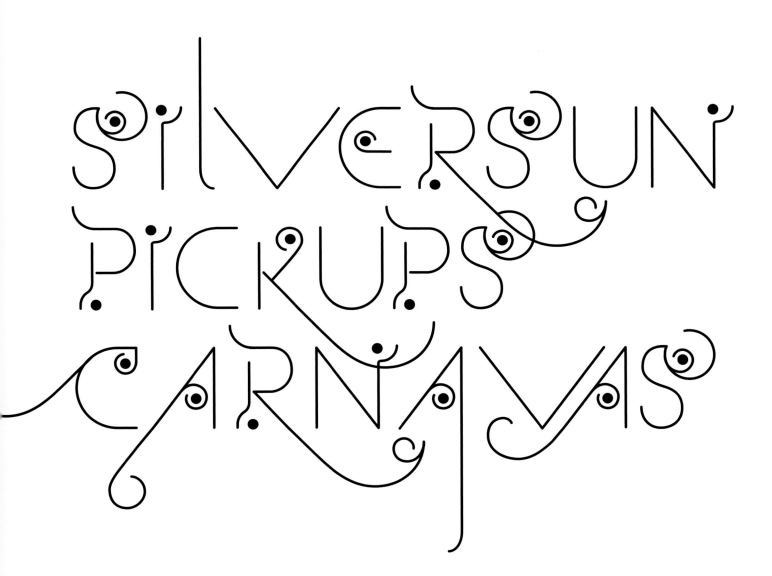

SILVERSUN PICKUPS / *CARNAVAS* / DANGERBIRD RECORDS / SMOG DESIGN / SARA CUMINGS / 2006

THE HIVES / INTERSCOPE RECORDS / HENRIK WALSE / 2005

# INTERVIEW WITH HENRIK WALSE

Self-taught, self-employed art director and designer Henrik Walse has been focusing on design for the music industry since he started in 1998. Henrik has created multiple logos, album covers, and posters for some of Sweden's hottest exports, including Sahara Hotnights, Danko Jones, The Hellacopters, and The Hives.

• What's your background?

I'm from Sweden. I live and work in Stockholm. I did not go to design school.

• How did you begin doing design for music?

Growing up skateboarding, I got in touch with a lot of people playing in bands. I started to do stuff for my friends, and some of them got really big, so I got pretty well-known in the music industry.

• It looks like you're the "go-to" guy for rock design in Sweden, but you also do a lot for U.S.- and U.K.-based labels like Universal, Virgin, and EMI. How is it working from a distance? Do you feel like we've gotten to the point where designers can work remotely from home, or do you spend a lot of time traveling for meetings and photo shoots?

It's really easy to work long-distance now. The only thing is the photo shoots. I really like to be part of those, so I have to travel some. I had my office in New York for a while and worked mostly with Swedish clients without problems. I guess you can be wherever there's a good Internet connection. But it is easier to be at my office in Stockholm, where I have tons of material, books, etc., for inspiration.

• Can you tell me a little about your process when you're developing a new logo for a band? Do you listen to the music over and over? Do you look through logo books for ideas? Do you look through your CD collection? Do you go to the music store?

I mostly look through old magazines. I'm really good at seeing things in stuff that doesn't look that good. Then I try to incorporate my own thoughts in the stuff I find. A lot of my inspiration also comes from traveling. And of course collecting old records.

• Who has been your favorite band to work with so far?

I must say The Hives. They have such great ideas to work from. But I also like to work with bands that leave the design completely up to me. The Hives are really cool about design. They always tell me I have to do stupid simple design, so it looks like they could've done it by themselves. I'm really into the designs of underground power pop and New Wave singles from the late '70s early '80s. Most of that stuff is really simple and "stupid" design and I just love it!

• What do you do if you're hired to do work for a band, and you really don't like their music? Does it make it harder?

That happens a lot because I'm not really into modern music at all.

• So we've already lost most of the great album art, and we're quickly seeing CDs die out too in favor of MP3s. Do you think the art of the band logo is going to be disappearing too?

The band has to promote themselves through a strong graphic profile. I think the artwork will always be there. The only thing that changes is the money involved, I guess. And that sucks.

SAHARA HOTNIGHTS / BMG UK / HENRIK WALSE / 2003

SAHARA HOTNIGHTS / BMG UK / HENRIK WALSE / 2001

SAHARA HOTNIGHTS / BMG UK / HENRIK WALSE / 2004

CAPTAIN MURPHY / WILD KINGDOM RECORDS / HENRIK WALSE / 2007

SONGS OF SOIL / STARTRACKS / HENRIK WALSE / 2001

DEATH CAB FOR CUTIE / T-SHIRT LOGO / JASON MUNN / 2005

MADONNA / *MUSIC* / MAVERICK RECORDS / KEVIN REAGAN / 2000

# M A D O N N A

MADONNA  /  SIRE RECORDS  /  CARIN GOLDBERG  /  1983

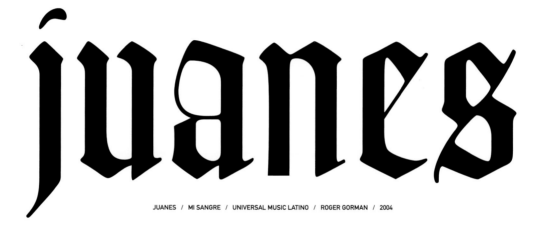

FALCO

FALCO / *NACHTFLUG* / A&M RECORDS / 1992

juanes

JUANES / MI SANGRE / UNIVERSAL MUSIC LATINO / ROGER GORMAN / 2004

eURYTHMICs

EURYTHMICS / *TOUCH* / RCA RECORDS / LAURENCE STEPHENS / 1983

FALCO / *EINZELHAFT* / A&M RECORDS / STEFAN WEBER / 1982

# MARIE OSMOND

MARIE OSMOND / *PAPER ROSES* / COLUMBIA RECORDS / SAUL SAGET / 1973

# WHAM!

WHAM! / COLUMBIA RECORDS / 1984

# naked eyes

NAKED EYES / EMI RECORDS / 1983

GIRLS
ALOUD

THE CARPENTERS / A&M RECORDS / CRAIG BRAUN AND ASSOCIATES / 1971

AIR SUPPLY / ARISTA RECORDS / 1982

# COLDPLAY

COLDPLAY / PARLOPHONE RECORDS / 2000

# vanessa paradis

VANESSA PARADIS / REMARK RECORDS / HUART-CHOLLEY / 1992

# Peter Paul and Mary

PETER PAUL AND MARY / *IN THE WIND* / WARNER BROS. RECORDS / MILTON GLASSER / 1962

**\*NSYNC**

\*NSYNC / RCA RECORDS / KIM BIGGS / 1998

**ABBA**

ABBA / POLAR MUSIC / 1973

*will young*

WILL YOUNG / SONY BMG MUSIC / STYLOROUGE / 2005

# VILLAGE PEOPLE

VILLAGE PEOPLE / *CAN'T STOP THE MUSIC* / CASABLANCA RECORDS / 1980

CULTURE CLUB / *KISSING TO BE CLEVER* / VIRGIN RECORDS / NICK EGAN & JAKI GRAHAM / 1982

BANANARAMA / *DEEP SEA SKIVING* / LONDON RECORDS / 1983

MEN WITHOUT HATS / MCA / 1980

DARYL JOHN

HALL & OATES / *BIG BAM BOOM* / RCA RECORDS / MICK HAGGERTY / 1984

PABLO CRUISE / *A PLACE IN THE SUN* / A&M RECORDS / CHRIS FRAYNE / 1977

a·ha

A-HA / *ANALOGUE* / UNIVERSAL INTERNATIONAL / MARTIN KVAMME / 2005

MEN AT WORK / *CARGO* / COLUMBIA RECORDS / 1982

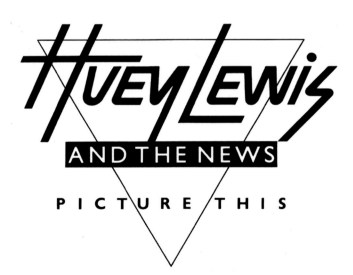

HUEY LEWIS AND THE NEWS / *PICTURE THIS* / CHRYSALIS RECORDS / NORMAN MOORE / 1982

BARRY MANILOW / *GREATEST HITS* / ARISTA RECORDS / DONN DAVENPORT / 1978

THE BEACH BOYS / LOGO FOR CONCERT POSTER / ART CHANTRY / 2002

THE MONKEES / NICK LOBIANCO / 1966

THE BEACH BOYS / *PET SOUNDS* / CAPITOL RECORDS / TOMMY STEELE / 1966

CHER / *LIVING PROOF* / WARNER BROS. RECORDS / SMOG DESIGN / 2006

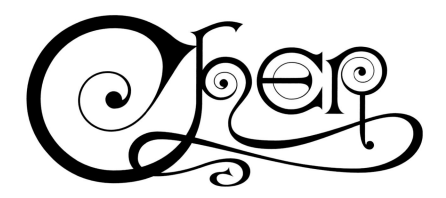

CHER / *LIVING PROOF* / WARNER BROS. RECORDS / SMOG DESIGN / 2006

BRANDY / *BEST OF* / ATLANTIC RECORDS / SMOG DESIGN / SARA CUMINGS / 2005

CHER / *LIVING PROOF* / WARNER BROS. RECORDS / SMOG DESIGN / 2006

GERI HALLIWELL / EMI RECORDS / STYLOROUGE / 2005

PUSSYCAT DOLLS / A&M RECORDS / SMOG DESIGN / GLEN NAKASAKO / 2005

JANET JACKSON / *JANET.* / VIRGIN RECORDS / LEN PELTIER / 1993

JANET JACKSON / *DAMITA JO* / VIRGIN RECORDS / SMOG DESIGN / 2004

JANET JACKSON / *ALL FOR YOU* / VIRGIN RECORDS / SMOG DESIGN / GLEN NAKASAKO & JERI HEIDEN / 2002

BRITNEY SPEARS / *...BABY ONE MORE TIME* / JIVE RECORDS / JACKIE MURPHY / 1999

CELINE DION / COLUMBIA RECORDS / 1993

ENYA / REPRISE RECORDS / LAURENCE DUNMORE / 1988

PINK / *I'M NOT DEAD* / LA FACE RECORDS / SMOG DESIGN / GLEN NAKASAKO / 2006

JENNIFER LOPEZ / *J.LO* / EPIC RECORDS / SLANG INC / 2001

BEASTIE BOYS / *LICENSED TO ILL* / DEF JAM RECORDINGS / CEY ADAMS / 1986

BEASTIE BOYS / *TO THE 5 BOROUGHS* / CAPITOL RECORDS / CEY ADAMS / 2004

BEASTIE BOYS / CAPITOL RECORDS / CEY ADAMS / 2004

**BLACK SHEEP**

BLACK SHEEP / *A WOLF IN SHEEP'S CLOTHING* / MERCURY RECORDS / 1991

JAY-Z / *VOL 3... LIFE AND TIMES OF S. CARTER* / ROC-A-FELLA RECORDS / 1999

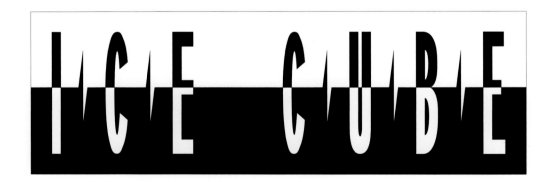

ICE CUBE / PRIORITY RECORDS / 1991

# LIL' WAYNE

LIL' WAYNE / CASH MONEY RECORDS / 2001

# N★E★R★D

N•E•R•D / VIRGIN RECORDS / BLK/MRKT / 2001

BUCK THE WORLD

YOUNG BUCK / *STRAIGHT OUTTA CASHVILLE* / G UNIT/INTERSCOPE / SLANG INC / 2007

QUANTIC  /  TRU THOUGHTS RECORDINGS  /  2004

# THE ROOTS

THE ROOTS  /  REMEDY RECORDINGS  /  1993

THE BLACK EYED PEAS  /  *MONKEY BUSINESS*  /  A&M RECORDS  /  SHEPARD FAIREY  /  2005

CHINGY / *POWERBALLIN'* / CAPITOL RECORDS / 2004

CYPRESS HILL / *STONED RAIDERS* / COLUMBIA RECORDS / SOUL ASSASSINS STUDIOS / 2001

TONE-LŌC / DELICIOUS VINYL / 1988

THE BOOGIE BOYS / *DEALIN' WITH LIFE* / CAPITOL RECORDS / 1986

WHODINI / JIVE RECORDS / 1983

N.W.A / *STRAIGHT OUTTA COMPTON* / RUTHLESS RECORDS / 1988

# GRANDMASTER FLASH & THE FURIOUS FIVE

GRANDMASTER FLASH & THE FURIOUS FIVE / *THE MESSAGE* / SUGAR HILL RECORDS / 1982

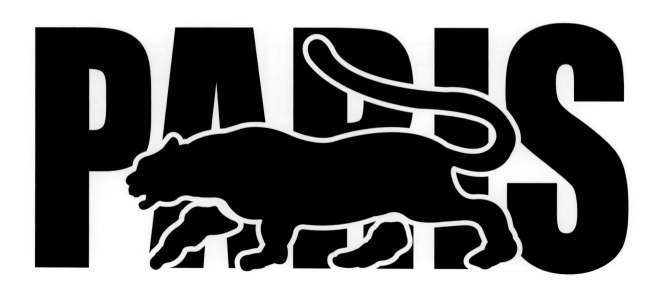

PARIS / TOMMY BOY MUSIC / 1990

MIKE JONES / ASYLUM RECORDS / 2005

THE GAME / *THE DOCUMENTARY* / AFTERMATH ENTERTAINMENT / 2006

YING YANG TWINS / TVT RECORDS / 2003

50 CENT / *POWER OF THE DOLLAR* / COLUMBIA RECORDS / SLANG INC / 1999

PUBLIC ENEMY / DEF JAM RECORDINGS / HAZE & CHUCK D / 1987

MC LYTE / *LYTE AS A ROCK* / FIRST PRIORITY MUSIC / BOB DEFRIN / 1988

RUN DMC  /  PROFILE RECORDS  /  1988

L.L. COOL J  /  *BIGGER & DEFFER*  /  DEF JAM RECORDINGS  /  ERIC HAZE  /  1987

HIEROGLYPHICS / HIEROGLYPHICS IMPERIUM RECORDINGS / DEL THA FUNKEE HOMOSAPIEN / 1997

JURASSIC 5 / INTERSCOPE RECORDS / CHALI 2NA / 1997

2PAC / *STRICTLY 4 MY N.I.G.G.A.Z.* / INTERSCOPE RECORDS / 1993

2PAC / *RESURRECTION* / INTERSCOPE / 2003

DJ SHADOW / *ENDTRODUCING.....* / MO' WAX / 1996

SIR MIX-A-LOT / DEF AMERICAN RECORDINGS / 1992

NAS / *IT WAS WRITTEN* / COLUMBIA RECORDS / AIMÉE MACAULEY / 1996

NAS / *ILLMATIC* / COLUMBIA RECORDS / AIMÉE MACAULEY / 1994

DMX / *YEAR OF THE DOG...AGAIN* / SONY URBAN MUSIC / CHRIS FELDMANN / 2006

D12 / SHADY RECORDS / MR. CARTOON / 2000

FOXY BROWN / *BROKEN SILENCE* / DEF JAM RECORDINGS / SLANG INC / 2001

RICH BOY / INTERSCOPE / SLANG INC / 2007

LLOYD BANKS  /  *THE ROTTEN APPLE*  /  G UNIT/INTERSCOPE  /  SLANG INC  /  2006

TONY YAYO  /  *THOUGHTS OF A PREDICATE FELON*  /  G UNIT/INTERSCOPE  /  SLANG INC  /  2005

# Tha Doggfather
## Snoop Doggy Dogg

SNOOP DOGGY DOGG / *THA DOGGFATHER* / DEATH ROW RECORDS / GEORGE PRYCE / 1996

# Fugees

FUGEES / *THE SCORE* / RUFFHOUSE RECORDS / 1996

BONE THUGS-N-HARMONY / RUTHLESS RECORDS / 1994

JA RULE / *EXODUS* / DEF JAM RECORDINGS / 2005

# TALIB KWELI
# THE BEAUTIFUL STRUGGLE

TALIB KWELI / *THE BEAUTIFUL STRUGGLE* / RAWKUS RECORDS / MORNING BREATH INC. / 2005

# kanYeWest
### late registration

KANYE WEST / *LATE REGISTRATION* / ROC-A-FELLA RECORDS / MORNING BREATH INC. / 2006

# EMINƎM

EMINEM / *THE MARSHALL MATHERS LP* / INTERSCOPE RECORDS / MORNING BREATH INC. / 2000

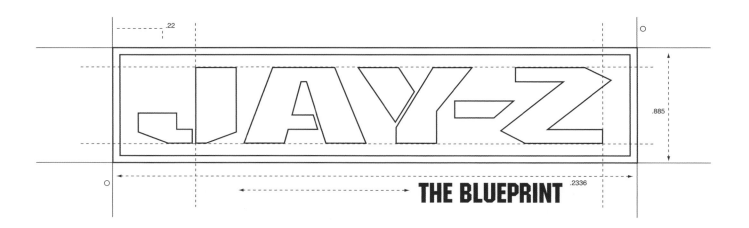

JAY-Z / *THE BLUEPRINT* / ROC-A-FELLA RECORDS / MORNING BREATH INC. / 2000

DJ QBERT / *WAVE TWISTERS* / THUD RUMBLE RECORDS / MORNING BREATH INC. / 2000

BLACKALICIOUS / *THE CRAFT* / ANTI- RECORDS / 2005

DADDY YANKEE / *BARRIO FINO* / EL CARTEL RECORDS / CARLOS PEREZ & MARK B. ALLEN / 2004

SAGE FRANCIS

SAGE FRANCIS / EPITAPH RECORDS / 2005

WU-TANG CLAN / LOUD RECORDS / MATHEMATICS / 1993

In a February 2007 interview with Brian Kayser for the Web site HipHopGame.com, producer Mathematics offered an account of his design process for creating his instantly iconic logo for the Wu-Tang Clan:

"[The logo] just popped up. Really, it was done in one night. When RZA was still on Tommy Boy, that's when the Wu-Tang idea really came. I did a sticker for him in graffiti that was a "W." That's when the first "W" really came. We were saying how we needed something that would really stick in people's heads. When you see Batman's symbol, you know Batman is coming. Everybody knows that Batman is coming. There's no words. You just know that Bruce Wayne is coming. We wanted something like that. That's why we had the "W." I was in the lab when I was still living in 40 Projects and sat down and that's what I drew. They came and got me when I was on a job site. I was doing carpentry at the time. When they saw it, they were like, 'This is it.' That was it."

VANILLA ICE / SBK RECORDS / 1990

EPMD / PRIORITY RECORDS / ERIC HAZE / 1988

MASE / *WELCOME BACK* / BAD BOY ENTERTAINMENT / 2004

# THE SYMBOL

The artist currently known as Prince was born Prince Rogers Nelson in 1958. But on his thirty-fifth birthday in 1993, Prince announced that his public life under that name was over. From that moment on, he wanted the press, his record label, and everyone else to refer to him by using an unpronounceable symbol that had appeared on his album covers and elsewhere since 1982. Visually, this icon seemed to be a stylized take on a combination of the traditional symbols for male and female. During negotiations regarding the release of Prince's next album, a battle ensued between Warner Bros. and Prince about the artistic and financial control of Prince's output. When the name change was announced, no reasons were given. Popular consensus was that he was just having a superstar tantrum. At the time, Prince appeared in public with the word "SLAVE" written on his cheek. On his Web site, The Dawn, Prince went on to explain the name change:

> "The first step I have taken towards the ultimate goal of emancipation from the chains that bind me to Warner Bros. was to change my name from Prince to ⚥. Prince is the name that my Mother gave me at birth. Warner Bros. took the name, trademarked it, and used it as the main marketing tool to promote all of the music that I wrote. The company owns the name Prince and all related music marketed under Prince. I became merely a pawn used to produce more money for Warner Bros. . .

> "I was born Prince and did not want to adopt another conventional name. The only acceptable replacement for my name, and my identity, was a symbol with no pronunciation, that is a representation of me and what my music is about. This symbol is present in my work over the years; it is a concept that has evolved from my frustration; it is who I am. It is my name."

Prince ceased using the symbol in 2000 after six albums and returned to using "Prince" again when his publishing contract had been fulfilled with Warner Bros. In a press conference stating that he was now free from undesirable relationships associated with the name "Prince," he formally reverted to his original name. He still occasionally uses the symbol as a logo and on album artwork and continues to play a ⚥-shaped guitar.

THE ARTIST FORMERLY KNOWN AS PRINCE   /   WARNER BROS. RECORDS   /   1993

PRINCE / *PURPLE RAIN* / WARNER BROS. RECORDS / 1984

COMMODORES / MOTOWN RECORDS / TOM NIKOSEY / 1977

STEVIE WONDER / *HOTTER THAN JULY* / TAMLA RECORDS / AL HARPER / 1980

THE POINTER SISTERS / RCA RECORDS / 1986

PATTI LABELLE / *WINNER IN YOU* / MCA RECORDS / ANN FIELD / 1986

CHAKA KHAN / *CHAKA* / WARNER BROS. RECORDS / TOM DRENNON / 1987

DIANA ROSS / *WHY DO FOOLS FALL IN LOVE* / RCA RECORDS / 1981

DONNA SUMMER / CASABLANCA RECORDS / TOM NIKOSEY / 1978

# MARY J BLIGE

MJB

MARY J BLIGE / *THE BREAKTHROUGH* / GEFFEN RECORDS / 2005

TYRESE / RCA RECORDS / 2001

ASHANTI / *CHAPTER 2* / DEF JAM RECORDINGS / ANDY WEST / 2003

PARLIAMENT / *MOTHERSHIP CONNECTION* / CASABLANCA RECORDS / GRIBBITT / 1975

TWEET / ELEKTRA RECORDS / 2002

TINA TURNER / *BREAK EVERY RULE* / CAPITOL RECORDS / STYLOROUGE / 1986

Boyz II Men

BOYZ II MEN / MOTOWN RECORDS / 1991

DES'REE / *DREAM SOLDIER* / SONY BMG RECORDS / STYLOROUGE / 2003

OHIOPLAYERS

OHIO PLAYERS / *FIRE* / MERCURY RECORDS / 1974

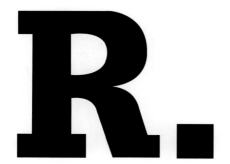

R. KELLY / *R.* / JIVE RECORDS / 1998

FLOETRY / DREAMWORKS RECORDS / GIANT2 / 2005

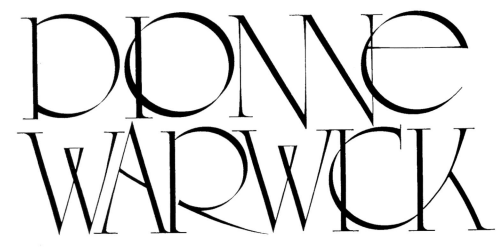

DIONNE WARWICK / PICCADILLY RECORDS / ART CHANTRY / 1980

WAR / UNITED ARTISTS RECORDS / BOB CATO / 1971

AVERAGE WHITE BAND / ATLANTIC RECORDS / ALAN GORRIE & TIM BRUCKNER / 1974

SNUFF / CURB RECORDS / SUZY BUNCH / 1982

# CASH

JOHNNY CASH / AMERICAN RECORDINGS / CHRISTINE CANO / 1995

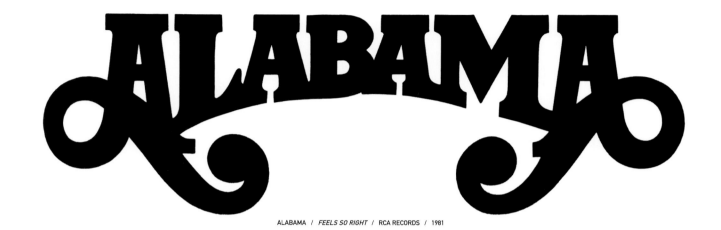

ALABAMA / *FEELS SO RIGHT* / RCA RECORDS / 1981

THE OAK RIDGE BOYS / *ROOM SERVICE* / ABC RECORDS / GERARD HUERTA / 1978

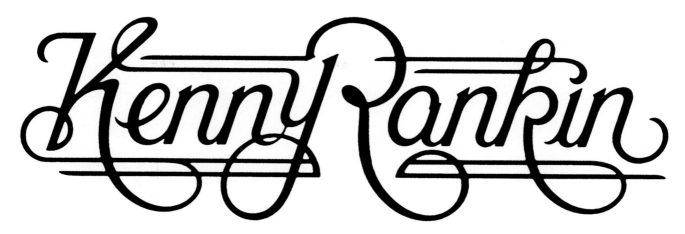

KENNY RANKIN / *AFTER THE ROSES* / ATLANTIC RECORDS / PACIFIC EYE & EAR / 1980

DON WILLIAMS / *ESPECIALLY FOR YOU* / MCA RECORDS / 1981

KENNY ROGERS / UNITED ARTISTS RECORDS / MICHAEL MANOOGIAN / 1976

T.G. SHEPPARD / *GREATEST HITS* / WARNER BROS. RECORDS / GLENN PARSONS / 1983

JESSI COLTER / *I'M JESSI COLTER* / CAPITOL RECORDS / ROY KOHARA / 1975

JOHN DENVER / *BACK HOME AGAIN* / RCA RECORDS / GRIBBITT! / 1974

LARRY GATLIN / *STRAIGHT AHEAD* / COLUMBIA RECORDS / JOHN YOUSSI / 1979

DIXIE CHICKS / *WIDE OPEN SPACES* / MONUMENT RECORDS / TRACY BASKETTE-FLEANER & BILL JOHNSON / 1998

CHET ATKINS / *BEST OF* / RCA RECORDS / 1964

ALABAMA / *MOUNTAIN MUSIC* / RCA RECORDS / DAVID HOGAN DESIGN / 1982

JOHN DENVER / *I WANT TO LIVE* / RCA RECORDS / GRIBBITT! / 1977

WILLIE NELSON / *SONGS* / LOST HIGHWAY RECORDS / T42 DESIGN / 2005

JOHN STEWART / *BOMBS AWAY DREAM BABIES* / RSO RECORDS / JACK UPSTON / 1979

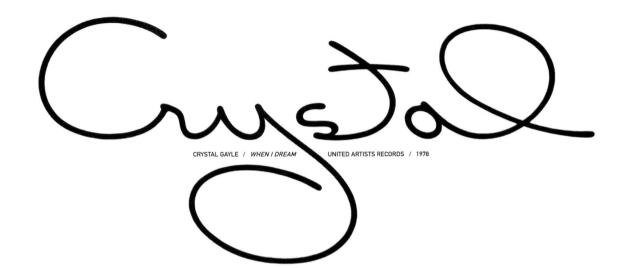

CRYSTAL GAYLE / *WHEN I DREAM*    UNITED ARTISTS RECORDS / 1978

DOLLY PARTON / *HERE YOU COME AGAIN* / RCA RECORDS / MICHAEL MANOOGIAN / 1977

# The Charlie Daniels Band

THE CHARLIE DANIELS BAND / *ME AND THE BOYS* / EPIC RECORDS / 1985

THE MARSHALL TUCKER BAND / *CAROLINA DREAMS* / CAPRICORN RECORDS / BILL FRANKS / 1977

AIR / *THE VIRGIN SUICIDES* / VIRGIN RECORDS / 2000

# AIR

AIR  /  *10 000 HZ LEGEND*  /  ASTRALWERKS RECORDS  /  2001

BAH SAMBA / ESTEREO RECORDINGS / RED DESIGN UK INC. / 2002

APHEX TWIN / *SELECTED AMBIENT WORKS 85-92* / APOLLO RECORDS / 1992

LO-FIDELITY ALLSTARS / *HOW TO OPERATE WITH A BLOWN MIND* / SKINT RECORDS / RED DESIGN UK INC. / 1998

KRAFTWERK / PHILIPS MUSIC / RALF HÜTTER / 1970

# nitzer ebb

NITZER EBB / MUTE RECORDS / 2006

BASEMENT JAXX  /  XL RECORDINGS  /  1999

DAFT PUNK / VIRGIN RECORDS / GUY-MANUEL DE HOMEM-CHRISTO / 1996

THE CHEMICAL BROTHERS / ASTRALWERKS RECORDS / 1995

KMFDM

KMFDM / *WHAT DO YOU KNOW, DEUTSCHLAND?* / Z RECORDS / 1986

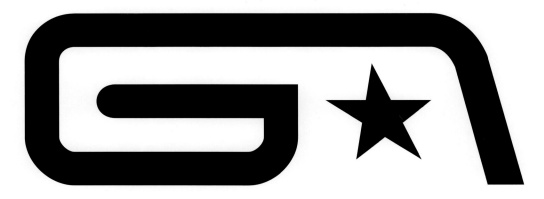

GROOVE ARMADA / *VERTIGO* / JIVE RECORDS / 1999

RÖYKSOPP / *ONLY THIS MOMENT* / ASTRALWERKS RECORDS / 2005

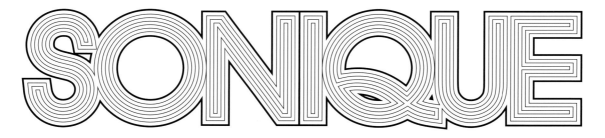

SONIQUE / *BORN TO BE FREE* / SERIOUS RECORDS / 2003

BARRAGE / *HERO OR DIRT* / FERAL MUSIC / SOPP COLLECTIVE / 2005

# deep forest

DEEP FOREST / *BOHEME* / COLUMBIA RECORDS / 1995

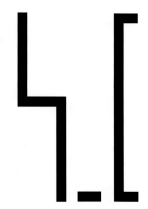

SUPER_COLLIDER / *RAW DIGITS* / RISE ROBOTS RISE / RED DESIGN UK LTD. / 2004

JAKATTA / *MY VISION* / MINISTRY OF SOUND NORDIC / STYLOROUGE / 2002

THE TAB TWO / VIRGIN RECORDS / KARLSSONWILKER INC. / 1997

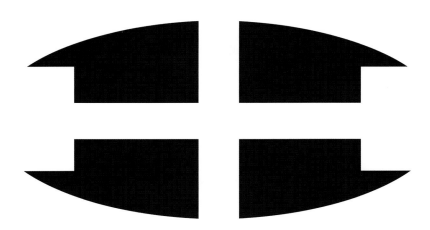

HATTLER / BASSBALL RECORDINGS / KARLSSONWILKER INC. / 2004

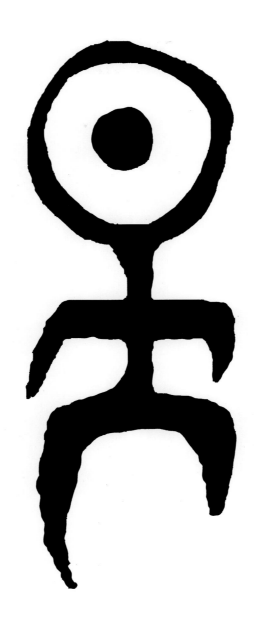

EINSTÜRZENDE NEUBAUTEN  /  ZICK ZACK RECORDS  /  1981

# The WAILING WAILERS

THE WAILING WAILERS / STUDIO ONE RECORDS / 1965

BOB MARLEY & THE WAILERS / *UPRISING* / ISLAND RECORDS / NEVILLE GARRICK / 1980

H.R. / *ANTHOLOGY* / SST RECORDS / 1998

JIMMY CLIFF / *THE HARDER THEY COME* / MANGO RECORDS / JOHN BRYANT / 1972

MAXI PRIEST / *INTENTIONS* / 10 RECORDS / STYLOROUGE / 1986

Toots & the Maytals

TOOTS & THE MAYTALS / *FUNKY KINGSTON* / ISLAND RECORDS / VISUALEYES / 1975

UB40

UB40 / VIRGIN RECORDS / 1980

MATISYAHU / *LIVE AT STUBB'S* / EPIC RECORDS / 2005

BEEF / PLAY IT AGAIN SAM / 2002

STEEL PULSE / ISLAND RECORDS / MARTIN FULLER / 1978

# BAND INDEX

# BAND INDEX

# BAND INDEX